Acknowledgements

I would like to thank all the people and nutritionists who participated from near and far in this project and particularly Josée Beaudet, Caroline Chevalt, Sylvie Laroche, Éliane Labonté, Claude-Henri Lapierre, Nathalie Sylvain, Anne-Marie Mitchell, Josiane Lanthier, Caroline Benoit, Marie-Chantale Tremblay, Marie-Claude Riel, Marie-Ève Trépanier, and Tracy Williams.

A special thanks to Sheila Bicknell, for her extraordinary work and her patience in translating this book and to Julie Demers and Nadine Brière for the revision. Thanks a lot, it's much appreciated!

Finally, a last word to those around me to express how much I appreciated the love and encouragement they showed me throughout this project. Thanks to Françoise Deslauriers and Pierre for all the love they give me.

Thanks to all the people who encourage me to create other recipe books.

With love, Marise

D1543778

Introduction

It has already been several years, one thing leading to another, that I have been working to complete a project that is very dear to me: putting together a recipe book to meet the requirements of a healthful and practical way of eating.

Nowadays, people are more and more informed and aware of the importance of good nutrition. However, the fast pace of the society in which we live results in it often becoming difficult to eat nutritiously. This book is intended for you and all those who would like to eat in a healthful way, but who are pressed for time. It is very easy to use and does not require great culinary skills. Even a child can create these recipes! Moreover, you will find that the majority of them are quick to prepare and will even save you more time if you double several recipes and then freeze the extra portions.

Eating nutritiously does not mean that we have to calculate everything we ingest to the letter. Nor does it mean that we have to consume only untransformed products or even to completely deprive ourselves of small treats. No, healthful eating is more about choosing a variety of healthy foods, and, sometimes, having small treats, all while listening to our body's needs. Healthful eating, regular physical activity, and a positive life philosophy is a combination for reaching harmony and well-being (the triangle of harmony).

Health begins with our food, and here is a practical tool to help you preciously preserve this treasure. With this book you will learn that it is possible to enjoy yourself while still eating in a healthful way.

I hope this book will become a part of your kitchen. Bon appétit, and most of all, I hope you find pleasure in healthful cooking and eating!

Marise Charron, Nutr., Dt.P., R.D.
Nutritionist

Healthy Eating Made Easy for the Whole Family

Marise Charron, Nutr., Dt.P., R.D.

Nutritionist

Translated by Sheila Bicknell, Nutr., Dt.P., R.D.

Harmonie Santé

Revised and corrected edition

Table of Contents

Appetizers and Beverages

Stuffed Zucchini

Preparation time: 5 minutes   Cooking time: 25 minutes
4 servings

Zucchini	4 small	
Zucchini pulp, chopped	variable quantity	
Shallot	1	
Cheese (20% m.f. or less), grated	60 ml	(1/4 cup)
Pepper, salt or no-salt shaker (pg. 155)	to taste	

1. Cut zucchini lengthwise.
2. Remove some pulp from the inside of the zucchini.
3. Chop the pulp.
4. Add the pulp to the other ingredients and mix well.
5. Stuff the zucchini and place on a greased cookie sheet.
6. Bake in the oven at 210°C (425°F) for approx. 20-25 minutes.
7. Serve as an entrée on a lettuce leaf.

One portion equals:
1/2 meat + 1 vegetable.

64 kilocalories   6 g proteins   5 g carbohydrates   3 g fat
10 mg cholesterol   2 g fiber   1 mg iron   133 mg calcium
36 mg magnesium   372 mg potassium   84 mg sodium

1

Cheese-Stuffed Mushrooms

Preparation time: 5 minutes   Cooking time: 15 minutes
4 servings

Mushrooms, medium, whole	8	
Green pepper, chopped	15 ml	(1 tbsp.)
Shallot, minced	1	
Cheese (20% m.f. or less), grated	30 ml	(2 tbsps.)
Pepper, salt or no-salt shaker (pg. 155)	to taste	

1. Wash and dry the mushrooms.
2. Remove the stems and finely chop them, keep the caps.
3. Add the chopped stems to the other ingredients and mix well.
4. Stuff the mushroom caps with this mixture.
5. Put on a greased cookie sheet.
6. Bake uncovered in the oven at 180ºC (350ºF) for approx. 15 minutes.
7. Serve as an entrée on a lettuce leaf.

One portion equals:
1/2 meat.

32 kilocalories   3 g proteins   2 g carbohydrates   2 g fat
5 mg cholesterol   1 g fiber   0 mg iron   58 mg calcium
6 mg magnesium   147 mg potassium   41 mg sodium

Cheese Bites

Preparation time: 5 minutes   Cooking time: 20 minutes
4 servings

Bread, whole wheat or your choice . . . . 4 slices cut in four
Ham, cooked, thinly sliced . . . . 2 slices cut in eight

Cheese (20% m.f. or less) . . . . 4 slices cut in four

1. Add the ham and the cheese of your choice onto the pieces of bread.
2. Put on a greased cookie sheet.
3. Bake uncovered in the oven at 180ºC (350ºF) for approx. 15-20 minutes.
4. Serve as an entrée on a lettuce leaf.

One portion equals:
1/2 meat + 1 bread.

70 kilocalories   3 g proteins   13 g carbohydrates   1 g fat
0 mg cholesterol   2 g fiber   1 mg iron   20 mg calcium
24 mg magnesium   71 mg potassium   149 mg sodium

Salmon Mousse

Preparation time: 65 minutes   Cooking time: none
4 servings

Gelatine, plain	1 envelope	(1 tbsp.)
Water	250 ml	(1 cup)
Salmon, flaked, drained	184 g	(1 x 6 1/2 oz can)
Cream cheese, light	60 ml	(1/4 cup)
Shallot, minced	1	
Red pepper, chopped	15 ml	(1 tbsp.)
Basil, parsley	a pinch of each	
Pepper, salt or no-salt shaker (pg. 155)	to taste	

1. Sprinkle the gelatine onto the water and let swell for approx. 5 minutes.
2. Heat to dissolve the gelatine (over low heat or in the microwave).
3. Add this mixture to the other ingredients.
4. Put through the blender to obtain a smooth texture.
5. Refrigerate for at least 1 hour.
6. Serve on rusks or other crackers.

One portion equals:
2 meats.

108 kilocalories   15 g proteins   1 g carbohydrate   5 g fat
40 mg cholesterol   0 g fiber   0 mg iron   23 mg calcium
16 mg magnesium   216 mg potassium   146 mg sodium

4

Light Cretons

Gelatine, plain	1 envelope	(1 tbsp.)
Water	60 ml	(1/4 cup)
Veal, beef, or horse, ground, lean	454 g	(1 pound)
Onion, chopped	1	
Celery, chopped	1 stalk	
Broth of your choice	250 ml	(1 cup)
Cinnamon	1 ml	(1/4 tsp.)
Nutmeg	1 ml	(1/4 tsp.)
Cloves, ground	a pinch	
Pepper, salt or no-salt shaker (pg. 155)	to taste	

1. Sprinkle the gelatine onto the water and let swell for approx. 5 minutes.
2. In a saucepan, cook the meat, onion, and celery without added fat for 5 minutes.
3. Add the remaining ingredients.
4. Cover and cook over low heat for approximately 25 minutes.
5. Add the thickened gelatine at the end of cooking.
6. If a smooth texture is desired, put all ingredients through a blender.
7. Place on small individual platters or on one large square platter.
8. Refrigerate or freeze.
9. Serve on rusks or other crackers.

One portion equals:
1 meat.

64 kilocalories   8 g proteins   1 g carbohydrate   3 g fat
31 mg cholesterol   0 g fiber   0 mg iron   12 mg calcium
12 mg magnesium   164 mg potassium   105 mg sodium

Soy Beverage

Preparation time: 35 minutes   Cooking time: 30 minutes
8 servings

Soybeans, white, uncooked	250 ml	(1 cup)
Water for soaking, enough to cover the beans . .	250 ml	(1 cup)
Hot water	2.0 L	(8 cups)
Brown sugar, sugar, honey, fructose or fruit purée .	10 ml	(2 tsps.)
Canola oil or linseed oil (optional)	10 ml	(2 tsps.)

1. Put the soybeans in a sealed dish.
2. Cover with water and leave soaking for approx. 24 hours in the refrigerator.
3. Heat 2 Liters of water in a pot.
4. Put the soybeans in the blender.
5. Add some hot water to help crush the soybeans.
6. Strain and put the crushed soybeans in the pot with the water.
7. Slowly bring to a boil, watch to prevent it boiling over.
8. Lower the heat and cover. Continue cooking for approx. 25 minutes.
9. Over a large bowl, pour this mixture through a strainer.
10. Add the honey and oil to your taste. Stir well.
11. Ask your nutritionist about enriching the milk with calcium, vitamin D, vitamin B_{12}...
12. Serve in a glass, with cereal, or to replace milk in your recipes.

One portion equals:
1/2 meat + 1/2 bread.

64 kilocalories   4 g proteins   5 g carbohydrates   3 g fat
0 mg cholesterol   0 g fiber   1 mg iron   68 mg calcium
23 mg magnesium   210 mg potassium   7 mg sodium

Fruit Egg~Nog

Preparation time: 2 minutes   Cooking time: none
4 servings

Eggs, very fresh 2
Milk (2% m.f. or less), very cold   . . . . 500 ml   (2 cups)
Brown sugar, sugar, honey, fructose or fruit purée . . 30 ml   (2 tbsps.)
Vanilla . . . . 2 ml   (1/2 tsp.)

Fruit of your choice (strawberries cut in two, bananas...) 500 ml   (2 cups)

1. Put all ingredients in a blender.
2. Serve immediately.

One portion equals:
1/2 meat + 1 fruit + 1/2 milk.

176 kilocalories   8 g proteins   26 g carbohydrates   5 g fat
11 mg cholesterol   2 g fiber   1 mg iron   175 mg calcium
28 mg magnesium   457 mg potassium   96 mg sodium

Quick Punch

Preparation time: 5 minutes   Cooking time: none
16 servings

Oranges, cold, peeled, sliced	2	
Fruit juice (orange, tropical, etc.)	2.0 L	(8 cups)
Cherries	125 ml	(1/2 cup)
Diet soft drink (diet 7-Up)	2.0 L	(8 cups)
Ice cubes	500 ml	(2 cups)
Your choice of alcohol (rum, vodka, etc)	beside the punch	

1. Add the first 3 ingredients to a punch bowl.
2. When it is time to serve, add the soft drink and ice cubes.
3. Serve with or without alcohol.

One portion equals:
1 fruit.

77 kilocalories   0 g protein   19 g carbohydrates   0 g fat
0 mg cholesterol   0 g fiber   0 mg iron   16 mg calcium
7 mg magnesium   141 mg potassium   7 mg sodium

8

Homemade Poultry Broth

Preparation time: 10 minutes   Cooking time: 2 hours
8 servings

Chicken or turkey carcass	1	
Water	2.0 L	(8 cups)
Celery, cut on a diagonal	1 stalk	
Onion, in pieces	1	
Carrots, in pieces	2	
Garlic, minced	1 clove	
Tarragon	5 ml	(1 tsp.)
Thyme, fresh	5 ml	(1 tsp.)
Pepper, salt or no-salt shaker (pg. 155)	to taste	

1. Place all ingredients in a saucepan.
2. Cover and cook over low heat for approx. 2 hours.
3. Pour the broth through a strainer.
4. Put the broth in the refrigerator.
5. Defat with a spoon when cool.
6. Use immediately or freeze.

One portion equals:
Bonus or 1/2 vegetable if vegetables kept.

24 kilocalories   1 g protein   4 g carbohydrates   0 g fat
2 mg cholesterol   1 g fiber   0 mg iron   15 mg calcium
7 mg magnesium   130 mg potassium   15 mg sodium

Beef or Veal Broth

Preparation time: 10 minutes   Cooking time: 2 hours
8 servings

Soup bone from beef or from veal	2	
Water, cold	2.0 L	(8 cups)
Celery, cut on a diagonal	1 stalk	
Celery leaves, chopped	30 ml	(2 tbsps.)
Onion, chopped	1	
Carrots, chopped	2	
Garlic	1 clove	
Basil, fresh, chopped	30 ml	(2 tbsps.)
Thyme, fresh	5 ml	(1 tsp.)
Pepper, salt or no-salt shaker (pg. 155)	to taste	

1. Place all ingredients in a saucepan.
2. Cover and cook over low heat for approx. 2 hours.
3. Pour the broth through a strainer.
4. Put the broth in the refrigerator.
5. Defat with a spoon when cool.
6. Use immediately or freeze.

One portion equals:
Bonus or 1/2 vegetable if vegetables kept.

28 kilocalories   2 g proteins   4 g carbohydrates   0 g fat
4 mg cholesterol   1 g fiber   0 mg iron   16 mg calcium
8 mg magnesium   143 mg potassium   21 mg sodium

Vegetable Soup

Preparation time: 15 minutes   Cooking time: 60 minutes
10 servings

Carrots, in round slices	2	
Celery, cut on a diagonal	2 stalks	
Onion, minced	1	
Green pepper, cubed	1	
Rutabaga, cubed	125 ml	(1/2 cup)
Cabbage, green, minced	250 ml	(1 cup)
Broth of your choice	750 ml	(3 cups)
Tomatoes, canned	540 ml	(1 x 19 oz can)
Tomato juice	1.36 L	(1 x 48 oz can)
Thyme, fresh	a pinch	
Basil, fresh	15 ml	(1 tbsp.)
Oregano, fresh	15 ml	(1 tbsp.)
Pepper, salt or no-salt shaker (pg. 155)	to taste	

1. Place all ingredients in a saucepan.
2. Cook over low heat for approx. 60 minutes.
3. Serve.

One portion equals:
1 vegetable.

41 kilocalories   2 g proteins   8 g carbohydrates   1 g fat
0 mg cholesterol   2 g fiber   1 mg iron   33 mg calcium
17 mg magnesium   324 mg potassium   272 mg sodium

11

Cabbage Soup

Preparation time: 15 minutes   Cooking time: 30 minutes
4 servings

Carrot, in small pieces	1	
Celery, cubed	1 stalk	
Onion, minced	1	
Cabbage, green, minced	500 ml	(2 cups)
Broth of your choice	1250 ml	(5 cups)
Thyme, fresh	5 ml	(1 tsp.)
Basil, fresh	15 ml	(1 tbsp.)
Oregano, fresh	5 ml	(1 tsp.)
Pepper, salt or no-salt shaker (pg. 155)	to taste	

1. Put all ingredients in a saucepan.
2. Cook over low heat for approx. 30 minutes.
3. Serve.

One portion equals:
1 vegetable.

63 kilocalories   5 g proteins   9 g carbohydrates   1 g fat
0 mg cholesterol   2 g fiber   2 mg iron   84 mg calcium
26 mg magnesium   470 mg potassium   1058 mg sodium

Pea Soup

Preparation time: 10 minutes   Cooking time: 3 hours
12 servings

Soup peas, dry, uncooked	500 ml	(2 cups)
Water	to cover beans	
Broth of your choice	3.0 L	(12 cups)
Onion, minced	1	
Celery, cut on a diagonal	1 stalk	
Carrot, in small pieces	1	
Bay leaf	1	
Savory, ground	2 ml	(1/2 tsp.)
Ham, in small cubes	60 ml	(1/4 cup)
Pepper, salt or no-salt shaker (pg. 155)	to taste	

1. Put the peas in a bowl and cover with water.
2. Leave the peas soaking for 6 to 8 hours or overnight.
3. Strain and rinse the peas. Throw away the soaking water.
4. In a saucepan, add the peas to the remaining ingredients.
5. Cover and let simmer for approx. 3 hours.
6. Serve.

One portion equals:
1/2 meat + 1/2 bread.

73 kilocalories   6 g proteins   9 g carbohydrates   1 g fat
3 mg cholesterol   2 g fiber   1 mg iron   35 mg calcium
28 mg magnesium   362 mg potassium   910 mg sodium

French Onion Soup

Preparation time: 10 minutes   Cooking time: 25 minutes
4 servings

Onion, minced	4	
Butter, non hydrogenated margarine, or oil	5 ml	(1 tsp.)
Broth of your choice	1.0 L	(4 cups)
Basil, fresh	15 ml	(1 tbsp.)
Thyme, fresh	5 ml	(1 tsp.)
Garlic powder	1 ml	(1/4 tsp.)
Pepper, salt or no-salt shaker (pg. 155)	to taste	
Bread, whole wheat, toasted	4 slices	
Cheese (20% m.f. or less), grated	250 ml	(1 cup)

1. Lightly brown the onions with fat in a saucepan.
2. Add some water or broth as needed.
3. Add the broth and seasonings.
4. Cook uncovered over low heat for approx. 20 minutes.
5. Pour into the bowls and cover with a toasted slice of whole wheat bread.
6. Top with cheese.
7. Broil in the oven for approx. 5 to 10 minutes.
8. Serve.

One portion equals:
1 meat + 1 vegetable + 1 fat + 1 bread + 1 milk.

358 kilocalories   27 g proteins   31 g carbohydrates   15 g fat
40 mg cholesterol   5 g fiber   2 mg iron   575 mg calcium
66 mg magnesium   563 mg potassium   1354 mg sodium

Lentil Soup

Preparation time: 10 minutes   Cooking time: 60 minutes
4 servings

Lentils, uncooked	125 ml	(1/2 cup)
Onion, minced	1	
Celery, cut on a diagonal	1 stalk	
Carrot, minced	1	
Tomato, in pieces	1	
Chicken broth, defatted	1250 ml	(5 cups)
Garlic powder, parsley, and cumin	a pinch of each	
Pepper, salt or no-salt shaker (pg. 155)	to taste	

1. Mix all ingredients in a saucepan.
2. Bring to a boil and then reduce the heat.
3. Cover and let simmer for approx. 60 minutes.
4. Serve.

One portion equals:
1 meat + 1 vegetable + 1 bread.

142 kilocalories   12 g proteins   22 g carbohydrates   1 g fat
0 mg cholesterol   4 g fiber   3 mg iron   52 mg calcium
46 mg magnesium   634 mg potassium   1056 mg sodium

Barley Soup

Preparation time: 10 minutes   Cooking time: 60 minutes
4 servings

Barley, hulled, soaked the night before	60 ml	(1/4 cup)
Water	250 ml	(1 cup)
Broth of your choice	750 ml	(3 cups)
Onion, chopped	1	
Carrot, in small pieces	1	
Celery, cut on a diagonal	1 stalk	
Bay leaf	1	
Thyme, fresh	5 ml	(1 tsp.)
Oregano, fresh	5 ml	(1 tsp.)
Garlic powder	1 ml	(1/4 tsp.)
Pepper, salt or no-salt shaker (pg. 155)	to taste	

1. Strain the soaked barley.
2. Place all ingredients in a saucepan.
3. Cover and let simmer over low heat for approx. 60 minutes.
4. Serve.

One portion equals:
1/2 vegetable + 1/2 bread.

67 kilocalories   4 g proteins   12 g carbohydrates   1 g fat
0 mg cholesterol   3 g fiber   1 mg iron   33 mg calcium
25 mg magnesium   258 mg potassium   637 mg sodium

16

Cream of Carrot Soup

Preparation time: 10 minutes   Cooking time: 35 minutes
4 servings

Carrots, in pieces	4	
Onion, minced	1	
Broth of your choice	750 ml	(3 cups)
Pepper, salt or no-salt shaker (pg. 155)	to taste	
Curry powder	2 ml	(1/2 tsp.)
Garlic powder	1 ml	(1/4 tsp.)
Milk (2% m.f. or less)	250 ml	(1 cup)
Flour, whole wheat	30 ml	(2 tbsps.)
Parsley, fresh, chopped	15 ml	(1 tbsp.)

1. Put the first 6 ingredients in a saucepan.
2. Cover and cook for approx. 30 minutes.
3. Purée in a blender.
4. Mix the milk and the flour without making lumps and add to the carrot mixture.
5. Let simmer for approx. 5 minutes.
6. Garnish with parsley and serve.

One portion equals:
2 vegetables + 1/4 milk.

112 kilocalories   6 g proteins   18 g carbohydrates   2 g fat
5 mg cholesterol   3 g fiber   1 mg iron   124 mg calcium
36 mg magnesium   559 mg potassium   683 mg sodium

Cream of Vegetable Soup

Preparation time: 15 minutes   Cooking time: 35 minutes
4 servings

Broccoli, raw, in florets	500 ml	(2 cups)
Onion, in pieces	1	
Carrots, in pieces	2	
Celery, cut on a diagonal	1 stalk	
Green pepper, in pieces	1	
Broth of your choice	750 ml	(3 cups)
Basil, fresh	15 ml	(1 tbsp.)
Thyme, fresh	5 ml	(1 tsp.)
Oregano, fresh	10 ml	(2 tsps.)
Pepper, salt or no-salt shaker (pg. 155)	to taste	
Milk (2% m.f. or less)	250 ml	(1 cup)
Flour, whole wheat	30 ml	(2 tbsps.)

1. Add the first 10 ingredients in a saucepan.
2. Cover and cook over medium heat for approx. 30 minutes.
3. Purée in a blender.
4. Mix the milk and the flour without making lumps
   and add to the vegetable mixture.
5. Let simmer for approx. 5 minutes.
6. Garnish with parsley and serve.

One portion equals:
2 vegetables + 1/2 milk.

124 kilocalories   8 g proteins   21 g carbohydrates   2 g fat
5 mg cholesterol   4 g fiber   2 mg iron   176 mg calcium
52 mg magnesium   721 mg potassium   690 mg sodium

18

Cream of Tomato Soup

Preparation time: 10 minutes   Cooking time: 25 minutes
4 servings

Tomato juice	750 ml	(3 cups)
Onion, in pieces	1	
Carrot, in pieces	1	
Potato, raw, in pieces	1	
Basil, fresh	15 ml	(1 tbsp.)
Oregano, fresh	15 ml	(1 tbsp.)
Thyme, fresh	5 ml	(1 tsp.)
Pepper, salt or no-salt shaker (pg. 155)	to taste	
Milk (2% m.f. or less)	250 ml	(1 cup)

1. Put the first 8 ingredients in a saucepan.
2. Cover and cook over medium heat for approx. 20 minutes.
3. Purée in a blender.
4. Add the milk.
5. Let simmer for approx. 5 minutes.
6. Garnish with parsley and serve.

One portion equals:
2 vegetables + 1/2 milk.

120 kilocalories   6 g proteins   23 g carbohydrates   2 g fat
5 mg cholesterol   4 g fiber   4 mg iron   163 mg calcium
54 mg magnesium   878 mg potassium   743 mg sodium

Cream of Spinach Soup

Preparation time: 10 minutes   Cooking time: 35 minutes
4 servings

Spinach, raw	750 ml	(3 cups)
Onion, in pieces	1	
Pear, fresh, peeled, in pieces	1	
Potato, raw, in pieces	1 medium	
Broth of your choice	500 ml	(2 cups)
Basil, fresh	15 ml	(1 tbsp.)
Oregano, fresh	10 ml	(2 tsps.)
Garlic powder	1 ml	(1/4 tsp.)
Thyme, fresh	5 ml	(1 tsp.)
Pepper, salt or no-salt shaker (pg. 155)	to taste	
Milk (2% m.f. or less)	250 ml	(1 cup)
Flour, whole wheat	15 ml	(1 tbsp.)

1. Add the first 10 ingredients in a saucepan.
2. Cover and cook over medium heat for approx. 30 minutes.
3. Purée.
4. Mix the milk and the flour without making lumps.
5. Add to vegetable mixture.
6. Let simmer for approx. 5 minutes.
7. Garnish with parsley and serve.

One portion equals:
2 vegetables + 1/2 milk.

127 kilocalories   7 g proteins   22 g carbohydrates   2 g fat
5 mg cholesterol   5 g fiber   4 mg iron   191 mg calcium
72 mg magnesium   760 mg potassium   486 mg sodium

Chicken Salad

Preparation time: 10 minutes   Cooking time: none
4 servings

Olive oil, canola oil or other	15 ml	(1 tbsp.)
Lemon juice	15 ml	(1 tbsp.)
Mayonnaise, light	15 ml	(1 tbsp.)
Ginger, fresh, chopped	15 ml	(1 tbsp.)
Garlic powder	1 ml	(1/4 tsp.)
Pepper, salt or no-salt shaker (pg. 155)	to taste	
Chicken, cubed	250 ml	(1 cup)
Raisins	15 ml	(1 tbsp.)
Celery, in pieces	125 ml	(1/2 cup)
Shallot, minced	1	
Carrot, grated	1	
Lettuce of your choice, in pieces	1.0 L	(4 cups)

1. Mix the first 6 ingredients in a small bowl (salad dressing).
2. Mix the remaining ingredients in another bowl.
3. Add the salad dressing.
4. Mix well.
5. Serve immediately.

One portion equals:
2 meats + 1 vegetable.

160 kilocalories   17 g proteins   8 g carbohydrates   7 g fat
41 mg cholesterol   2 g fiber   1 mg iron   47 mg calcium
23 mg magnesium   446 mg potassium   97 mg sodium

Caesar Salad

Preparation time: 15 minutes   Cooking time: none
4 servings

Garlic powder	1 ml	(1/4 tsp.)
Mustard, dried	1 ml	(1/4 tsp.)
Yogurt, plain (2% m.f. or less)	30 ml	(2 tbsps.)
Mayonnaise, light	30 ml	(2 tbsps.)
Lemon juice	30 ml	(2 tbsps.)
Worcestershire sauce	2 ml	(1/2 tsp.)
Parmesan cheese (20% m.f. or less), grated	60 ml	(1/4 cup)
Romaine lettuce, fresh, in pieces	1	
Shallot, minced	1	
Simulated bacon or crispy bacon	30 ml	(2 tbsps.)
Cheese (20% m.f. or less), grated	125 ml	(1/2 cup)
Croutons, plain	250 ml	(1 cup)

1. Mix the first 7 ingredients in a small bowl (salad dressing).
2. Mix the remaining ingredients in another bowl.
3. Add the salad dressing.
4. Mix well.
5. Serve immediately.

One portion equals:
1/2 meat + 1 vegetable + 1 fat + 1/2 milk.

175 kilocalories   11 g proteins   9 g carbohydrates   10 g fat
19 mg cholesterol   1 g fiber   1 mg iron   273 mg calcium
15 mg magnesium   89 mg potassium   365 mg sodium

Greek Salad

Preparation time: 20 minutes   Cooking time: none
4 servings

Olive oil	15 ml	(1 tbsp.)
Lemon juice	30 ml	(2 tbsps.)
Oregano, fresh	5 ml	(1 tsp.)
Garlic, minced	1 clove	
Pepper, salt or no-salt shaker (pg. 155)	to taste	
Red onion, sliced	1	
Broccoli, raw, in florets	250 ml	(1 cup)
Cauliflower, florets	250 ml	(1 cup)
Red pepper, in strips	1	
Tomato, in pieces	1	
Cucumber, English, in round slices	1/2	
Black olives, pitted	10 ml	(2 tsps.)
Feta cheese (20% m.f. or less), cubed	250 ml	(1 cup)

1. Mix the first 5 ingredients in a small bowl (salad dressing).
2. Mix the remaining ingredients in another bowl.
3. Add the salad dressing.
4. Mix well.
5. Serve immediately on your choice of lettuce leaf, if desired.

One portion equals:
2 vegetables + 2 fat + 1 milk.

268 kilocalories   12 g proteins   16 g carbohydrates   18 g fat
60 mg cholesterol   3 g fiber   2 mg iron   377 mg calcium
40 mg magnesium   457 mg potassium   788 mg sodium

Rice and Chickpea Salad

Preparation time: 20 minutes   Cooking time: none
4 servings

Olive oil, canola oil or other	15 ml	(1 tbsp.)
Lemon juice	15 ml	(1 tbsp.)
Basil, fresh	15 ml	(1 tbsp.)
Onion powder and garlic powder	a pinch of each	
Pepper, salt or no-salt shaker (pg. 155)	to taste	
Chickpeas, cooked, drained	540 ml	(1 x 19 oz can)
Brown rice, long grain, cooked	250 ml	(1 cup)
Shallot, minced	1	
Carrot, in small pieces	1/2	
Celery, chopped	1 stalk	
Green pepper, chopped	1/2	

1. Mix the first 5 ingredients in a small bowl (salad dressing).
2. Mix the remaining ingredients in another bowl.
3. Add the salad dressing.
4. Mix well.
5. Serve.

One portion equals:
1/2 meat + 1 vegetable + 1/2 fat + 2 breads.

254 kilocalories   10 g proteins   41 g carbohydrates   6 g fat
0 mg cholesterol   6 g fiber   3 mg iron   61 mg calcium
73 mg magnesium   400 mg potassium   22 mg sodium

Chinese Salad

Preparation time: 15 minutes   Cooking time: none
4 servings

Olive oil	15 ml	(1 tbsp.)
Lemon juice	15 ml	(1 tbsp.)
Soy sauce	30 ml	(2 tbsps.)
Sunflower seeds	60 ml	(1/4 cup)
Garlic, minced	1 clove	
Beansprouts, raw	500 ml	(2 cups)
Celery, cut on a diagonal	1 stalk	
Red pepper, in pieces	1/2	
Shallot, minced	1	
Spinach, raw	1.0 L	(4 cups)
Pepper, salt or no-salt shaker (pg. 155)	to taste	

1. Mix the first 5 ingredients in a small bowl (salad dressing).
2. Mix the remaining ingredients in another bowl.
3. Add the salad dressing.
4. Mix well.
5. Serve.

One portion equals:
1/2 meat + 2 vegetables + 2 fat.

153 kilocalories   8 g proteins   10 g carbohydrates   11 g fat
0 mg cholesterol   2 g fiber   3 mg iron   96 mg calcium
88 mg magnesium   635 mg potassium   480 mg sodium

Coleslaw

Preparation time: 15 minutes   Cooking time: none
4 servings

Mayonnaise, light	30 ml	(2 tbsps.)
Yogurt, plain (2% m.f. or less)	30 ml	(2 tbsps.)
Lemon juice	15 ml	(1 tbsp.)
Mustard, dried	a pinch	
Relish	5 ml	(1 tsp.)
Garlic powder	a pinch	
Parsley, fresh, chopped	5 ml	(1 tsp.)
Pepper, salt or no-salt shaker (pg. 155)	to taste	
Cabbage, finely chopped	500 ml	(2 cups)
Carrot, in small pieces	1	
Shallot, minced	1	

1. Mix the first 8 ingredients in a small bowl (salad dressing).
2. Mix the remaining ingredients in another bowl.
3. Add the salad dressing.
4. Mix well.
5. Serve.

One portion equals:
1 vegetable + 1/2 fat.

48 kilocalories   1 g protein   6 g carbohydrates   3 g fat
1 mg cholesterol   1 g fiber   0 mg iron   36 mg calcium
10 mg magnesium   182 mg potassium   69 mg sodium

Waldorf Salad

Mayonnaise, light	30 ml	(2 tbsps.)
Yogurt, plain (2% m.f. or less)	30 ml	(2 tbsps.)
Parsley, fresh, chopped	5 ml	(1 tsp.)
Pepper, salt or no-salt shaker (pg. 155)	to taste	
Red apples, diced	2	
Lemon juice	15 ml	(1 tbsp.)
Celery, in small pieces	1 stalk	
Cashew nuts	60 ml	(1/4 cup)
Spinach or romaine lettuce, pieces	1.0 L	(4 cups)

1. Mix the first 4 ingredients in a small bowl (salad dressing).
2. Mix the remaining ingredients in another bowl.
3. Add the salad dressing.
4. Mix well.
5. Serve immediately.

One portion equals:
1/2 meat + 1 vegetable + 1 fat + 1/2 fruit.

135 kilocalories   4 g proteins   17 g carbohydrates   7 g fat
1 mg cholesterol   3 g fiber   2 mg iron   85 mg calcium
75 mg magnesium   512 mg potassium   112 mg sodium

27

Tasty Salad

Preparation time: 15 minutes   Cooking time: none
4 servings

Mayonnaise, light	30 ml	(2 tbsps.)
Yogurt, plain (2% m.f. or less)	80 ml	(1/3 cup)
Basil, fresh, and dried mustard	a pinch of each	
Brown sugar, sugar, honey, fructose or fruit purée	5 ml	(1 tsp.)
Cashew nuts, chopped	15 ml	(1 tbsp.)
Pepper, salt or no-salt shaker (pg. 155)	to taste	
Romaine lettuce, fresh, in pieces, or other	1	
Green peas, uncooked, drained	284 ml	(1 x 10 oz can)
Shallot, minced	1	
Tomato, in pieces	1	
Cheese (20% m.f. or less), grated	125 ml	(1/2 cup)
Eggs, hard-boiled, in pieces	2	

1. Mix the first 6 ingredients in a small bowl (salad dressing).
2. Mix the remaining ingredients in another bowl.
3. Add the salad dressing.
4. Mix well.
5. Serve immediately.

One portion equals:
1 meat + 1 vegetable + 1 fat + 1 milk.

231 kilocalories   17 g proteins   13 g carbohydrates   13 g fat
12 mg cholesterol   0 g fiber 1 mg iron   311 mg calcium
38 mg magnesium   305 mg potassium   280 mg sodium

Egg Salad

Preparation time: 5 minutes   Cooking time: none
4 servings

Mayonnaise, light	60 ml	(1/4 cup)
Yogurt, plain (2% m.f. or less)	60 ml	(1/4 cup)
Green olives, small, minced	2	
Shallot, minced	1	
Parsley, fresh, chopped	30 ml	(2 tbsps.)
Pepper, salt or no-salt shaker (pg. 155)	to taste	
Eggs, hard-boiled, in pieces	4	
Celery, minced	1 stalk	
Green pepper, in small pieces	1/2	
Boston lettuce, or lettuce of your choice	1.0 L	(4 cups)

1. Mix the first 6 ingredients in a small bowl (salad dressing).
2. Mix the remaining ingredients in another bowl.
3. Add the salad dressing.
4. Mix well.
5. Serve immediately.

One portion equals:
1 meat + 1 vegetable + 1 fat.

145 kilocalories   7 g proteins   5 g carbohydrates   11 g fat
21 mg cholesterol   1 g fiber   1 mg iron   61 mg calcium
12 mg magnesium   181 mg potassium   196 mg sodium

Fondue Sauce

Preparation time: 7 minutes   Cooking time: none
6 servings

Cream cheese, light	125 ml	(1/2 cup)
Yogurt, plain (2% m.f. or less)	250 ml	(1 cup)
Mayonnaise, light	30 ml	(2 tbsps.)
Shallot, minced	1	
Pepper, salt or no-salt shaker (pg. 155)	to taste	
Onion powder and garlic powder	a pinch of each	

1. Mix all ingredients.
2. Use various fondue sauces.
3. Serve.

One portion equals:
1 fat + 1/4 milk.

77 kilocalories   3 g proteins   3 g carbohydrates   6 g fat
15 mg cholesterol   0 g fiber   0 mg iron   54 mg calcium
3 mg magnesium   78 mg potassium   189 mg sodium

Delicious Dip

Preparation time: 10 minutes   Cooking time: none
4 servings

Yogurt, plain (2% m.f. or less)	125 ml	(1/2 cup)
Cream cheese, light	125 ml	(1/2 cup)
Mayonnaise, light	15 ml	(1 tbsp.)
Shallot, minced	15 ml	(1 tbsp.)
Celery, chopped	15 ml	(1 tbsp.)
Red pepper, chopped	15 ml	(1 tbsp.)
Green pepper, chopped	15 ml	(1 tbsp.)
Mushrooms, chopped	15 ml	(1 tbsp.)
Basil, fresh	15 ml	(1 tbsp.)
Pepper, salt or no-salt shaker (pg. 155)	to taste	

1. Mix all ingredients with or without an electric mixer.
2. Serve with raw vegetables.

One portion equals:
1/2 meat + 1 fat + 1/4 milk.

107 kilocalories   5 g proteins   4 g carbohydrates   8 g fat
22 mg cholesterol   0 g fiber   0 mg iron   84 mg calcium
7 mg magnesium   148 mg potassium   262 mg sodium

All-Purpose Salad Dressing

Preparation time: 7 minutes   Cooking time: none
32 servings

Olive oil, canola oil or other	180 ml	(3/4 cup)
Orange juice or tropical juice	125 ml	(1/2 cup)
Lemon juice	60 ml	(1/4 cup)
Mustard, dried	5 ml	(1 tsp.)
Garlic powder	a pinch	
Onion powder	a pinch	
Paprika	a pinch	
Parsley, fresh, chopped	15 ml	(1 tbsp.)
Pepper, salt or no-salt shaker (pg. 155)	to taste	

1. Mix all ingredients.
2. Serve immediately or refrigerate.

One portion equals:
1 fat.

48 kilocalories   0 g protein   1 g carbohydrate   5 g fat
0 mg cholesterol   0 g fiber   0 mg iron   1 mg calcium
1 mg magnesium   12 mg potassium   0 mg sodium

Homemade Mayonnaise

Preparation time: 7 minutes   Cooking time: none
33 servings

Egg, very fresh	1	
Salt	2 ml	(1/2 tsp.)
Mustard, dried	1 ml	(1/4 tsp.)
Pepper, onion powder, garlic powder	a pinch of each	
Lemon juice	30 ml	(2 tbsps.)
Olive oil	250 ml	(1 cup)
Yogurt, plain (2% m.f. or less)	250 ml	(1 cup)

1. Mix the first 5 ingredients in a blender at slow speed.
2. Allow the mixer to work slowly and add the oil in a thin trickle (whitened mixture). Do not go too fast since the mayonnaise will become too runny.
3. Add the yogurt to make a light mayonnaise.
4. Serve.

One portion equals:
1 fat.

69 kilocalories   1 g protein   1 g carbohydrate   7 g fat
7 mg cholesterol   0 g fiber   0 mg iron   14 mg calcium
2 mg magnesium   21 mg potassium   35 mg sodium

33

Sauces

Preparation time: 5 minutes   Cooking time: 5 minutes
8 servings

WHITE SAUCE

Milk (2% m.f. or less)	250 ml	(1 cup)
Onion powder	1 ml	(1/4 tsp.)
Garlic powder	1 ml	(1/4 tsp.)
Flour of your choice	30 ml	(2 tbsps.)
Poultry or beef broth	5 ml	(1 tsp.)
Pepper, salt or no-salt shaker (pg. 155)	to taste	

WITH CHEESE   : Add 60 ml (1/4 cup) of your choice of cheese.
WITH EGGS   : Add 2 hard-boiled eggs in pieces.
WITH MUSHROOMS : Add 125 ml (1/2 cup) of cooked mushrooms.
WITH TOMATOES : Replace the milk with tomato juice.

1. Mix the ingredients without making lumps.
2. Bring to a boil while constantly mixing.
3. Cook over medium heat (preferably in a double-boiler) to the desired consistency.
4. Reduce the heat and let simmer for 5 minutes.
5. Add the desired variation.
6. Serve.

One portion equals:
1/4 bread.

24 kilocalories   1 g protein   3 g carbohydrates   1 g fat
2 mg cholesterol   0 g fiber   0 mg iron   40 mg calcium
5 mg magnesium   53 mg potassium   20 mg sodium

Gravy

Preparation time: 5 minutes   Cooking time: 5 minutes
4 servings

Beef broth or beef consommé . . . . 250 ml   (1 cup)
Flour, whole wheat or flour of your choice . . . . . 30 ml   (2 tbsps.)
Onion powder . . . . 2 ml   (1/2 tsp.)
Garlic powder . . . . 1 ml   (1/4 tsp.)
Pepper, salt or no-salt shaker (pg. 155) . . . . . . to taste

1. Mix the ingredients without making lumps.
2. Bring to a boil while constantly mixing.
3. Cook over medium heat (preferably in a double-boiler) to the desired consistency.
4. Reduce the heat and let simmer for 5 minutes.
5. Serve.

One portion equals:
1/4 bread.

19 kilocalories   1 g protein   3 g carbohydrates   0 g fat
0 mg cholesterol   0 g fiber   0 mg iron   6 mg calcium
7 mg magnesium   53 mg potassium   207 mg sodium

35

B.B.Q. Sauce

Preparation time: 5 minutes   Cooking time: 2 minutes
8 servings

Beef broth or beef consommé	60 ml	(1/4 cup)
Ketchup	125 ml	(1/2 cup)
Worcestershire sauce	5 ml	(1 tsp.)
Mustard, dried	2 ml	(1/2 tsp.)
Soy sauce	5 ml	(1 tsp.)
Lemon juice	30 ml	(2 tbsps.)
Onion powder	2 ml	(1/2 tsp.)
Garlic powder	1 ml	(1/4 tsp.)
Pepper, salt or no-salt shaker (pg. 155)	to taste	

1. Mix all ingredients.
2. Reheat for 2 minutes in the microwave oven if desired.
3. Serve cold or hot.

One portion equals:
1/4 bread.

20 kilocalories   0 g protein   5 g carbohydrates   0 g fat
0 mg cholesterol   0 g fiber   0 mg iron   5 mg calcium
5 mg magnesium   91 mg potassium   255 mg sodium

Main Meals

Beef or Veal Delight

Preparation time: 15 minutes   Cooking time: 2 hours
4 servings

Beef or veal, lean ground	454 g	(1 pound)
Onion, minced	1	
Cream of tomato soup	568 ml	(2 x 10 oz can)
Water	250 ml	(1 cup)
Green pepper, in thin strips	1	
Carrots, in round slices	2	
Celery, diced	4 stalks	
Rutabaga, cubed	125 ml	(1/2 cup)
Potatoes, raw, sliced	4	
Pepper, salt or no-salt shaker (pg. 155)	to taste	

1. In a saucepan, cook the ground meat with onion but with no added fat.
2. Put in a greased rectangular baking pan.
3. Mix all other ingredients in another bowl, add to the pan over the meat.
4. Cover and cook in the oven at 180ºC (350ºF) for approx. 2 hours.
5. Serve.

One portion equals:
2 meats + 2 vegetables + 1 bread.

233 kilocalories   21 g proteins   28 g carbohydrates   5 g fat
29 mg cholesterol   6 g fiber   6 mg iron   69 mg calcium
57 mg magnesium   1143 mg potassium   438 mg sodium

Beef or Veal Bourguignon

Preparation time: 20 minutes   Cooking time: 2 hours
4 servings

Beef or veal, cubed	454 g	(1 pound)
Garlic, minced	1 clove	
Carrots, in round slices	3 medium	
Celery, in pieces	2 stalks	
Onion, minced	1	
Beef broth	750 ml	(3 cups)
Red wine	125 ml	(1/2 cup)
Mushrooms, chopped	500 ml	(2 cups)
Green pepper, minced	1	
Thyme, fresh	15 ml	(1 tbsp.)
Basil, fresh	30 ml	(2 tbsps.)
Bay leaf	3	
Flour, whole wheat	15 ml	(1 tbsp.)
Red wine	125 ml	(1/2 cup)

1. Cook the first 5 ingredients in a pot with some broth for approx. 10 minutes.
2. Add the broth and the wine, cover and cook over low heat for approx.
   1 1/2 hours.
3. Mix the 7 other ingredients without making lumps.
4. Add this mixture to the remaining ingredients.
5. Continue cooking for approx. 30 minutes.
6. Serve.

One portion equals:
3 meats + 2 vegetables.

235 kilocalories   22 g proteins   12 g carbohydrates   7 g fat
39 mg cholesterol   2 g fiber   3 mg iron   55 mg calcium
49 mg magnesium   905 mg potassium   693 mg sodium

Special Shepherd's Pie

Preparation time: 20 minutes   Cooking time: 30 minutes
6 servings

Beef or veal, lean ground	454 g	(1 pound)
Onion, minced	1 medium	
Pepper	a pinch	
Onion powder and garlic powder	a pinch of each	
Corn, creamed or kernel	284 ml	(1 x 10 oz can)
Potatoes, cooked	4 medium	
Rutabaga, cubed	250 ml	(1 cup)
Carrots, cooked	2	
Milk (2% m.f. or less)	125 ml	(1/2 cup)
Pepper, salt, onion powder	to taste	
Paprika	a pinch	

1. Lightly cook the meat and the onion without added fat. Season.
2. Drain off the fat.
3. Put the mixture in a pan for the oven.
4. Add the corn to the mixture.
5. Purée the vegetables, adding the milk, pepper, salt, and onion powder.
6. Put the purée on top and sprinkle with paprika.
7. Bake in the oven uncovered at 180°C (350°F) for approx. 30 minutes.
8. Serve.

One portion equals:
2 meats + 1 vegetable + 2 breads.

255 kilocalories   20 g proteins   35 g carbohydrates   4 g fat
30 mg cholesterol   3 g fiber   2 mg iron   58 mg calcium
55 mg magnesium   902 mg potassium   224 mg sodium

Hamburger Surprise

Preparation time: 5 minutes   Cooking time: 10 minutes
4 servings

Beef or veal, lean ground	227 g	(1/2 pound)
Turkey, uncooked	227 g	(1/2 pound)
Worcestershire sauce	5 ml	(1 tsp.)
Onion, minced	1	
Cheese (20% m.f. or less), grated	60 ml	(1/4 cup)
Spinach, in small pieces	125 ml	(1/2 cup)
Garlic powder	a pinch	
Pepper, salt or no-salt shaker (pg. 155)	to taste	
Hamburger buns, whole wheat	4	
Lettuce of your choice, in pieces	to your taste	
Tomato, slices	1	

1. Mix the first 8 ingredients.
2. Form into 4 patties ready to cook.
3. Cook on the B.B.Q. or in a pan until the center is no longer pink.
4. Put in the hamburger buns.
5. Top with lettuce and tomatoes.
6. Serve with a portion of healthy fries (pg. 77) and a salad.

One portion equals:
3 meats + 1 1/2 breads + 1/2 milk.

320 kilocalories   31 g proteins   31 g carbohydrates   9 g fat
58 mg cholesterol   5 g fiber   4 mg iron   185 mg calcium
84 mg magnesium   617 mg potassium   456 mg sodium

Beef or Veal and Vegetable Stew

Preparation time: 15 minutes   Cooking time: 90 minutes
4 servings

Beef or veal, cubed	454 g	(1 pound)
Onion, minced	1	
Broth of your choice	750 ml	(3 cups)
Celery, in pieces	2 stalks	
Carrots, in round slices	4	
Mushrooms, sliced	250 ml	(1 cup)
Cabbage, in pieces	125 ml	(1/2 cup)
Rutabaga, cubed	125 ml	(1/2 cup)
Potatoes, sliced	4	
Worcestershire sauce	30 ml	(2 tbsps.)
Tomato paste	15 ml	(1 tbsp.)
Pepper, salt or no-salt shaker (pg. 155)	to taste	

1. In a pot, cook the meat cubes with onion without added fat for approx. 10 minutes.
2. Moisten with some broth or water as needed.
3. Add the broth.
4. Cover and cook over medium heat for approx. 50 minutes.
5. Add the 9 other ingredients.
6. Continue cooking uncovered for 20 to 30 minutes.
7. Serve.

One portion equals:
2 meats + 3 vegetables + 1 bread + 1/2 milk.

331 kilocalories   28 g proteins   42 g carbohydrates   7 g fat
39 mg cholesterol   11 g fiber   9 mg iron   165 mg calcium
103 mg magnesium   1955 mg potassium   858 mg sodium

Chinese Beef or Veal

Preparation time: 10 minutes   Cooking time: 20 minutes
4 servings

Beef, tender, strips	454 g	(1 pound)
Onion, minced	1	
Beef broth or other flavor	250 ml	(1 cup)
Flour, whole wheat	15 ml	(1 tbsp.)
Worcestershire sauce	2 ml	(1/2 tsp.)
Soy sauce, light	30 ml	(2 tbsps.)
Ginger, fresh, and garlic powder	to your taste	
Mushrooms, sliced	500 ml	(2 cups)
Red pepper, in strips	1	
Green pepper, in strips	1	
Celery, cut on a diagonal	1 stalk	
Broccoli, raw, in florets	250 ml	(1 cup)
Cauliflower, in florets	250 ml	(1 cup)
Parsley, fresh, chopped	30 ml	(2 tbsps.)

1. In a pot, cook the meat with onion but no fat over high heat for approx. 10 minutes.
2. Moisten with some broth or water as needed.
3. Mix the next 12 ingredients without lumps.
4. Add this mixture to the first mixture (meat and onion).
5. Cook uncovered over medium heat for approx. 10 minutes.
6. Serve with rice if desired.

One portion equals:
3 meats + 2 vegetables.

230 kilocalories   29 g proteins   16 g carbohydrates   6 g fat
43 mg cholesterol   3 g fiber   3 mg iron   51 mg calcium
55 mg magnesium   1060 mg potassium   713 mg sodium

Beef or Veal Hot Pot

Preparation time: 10 minutes   Cooking time: 30 minutes
4 servings

Beef or veal, lean ground	454 g	(1 pound)
Onion, minced	1	
Celery, in pieces	2 stalks	
Potatoes, raw, in pieces	4 medium	
Yellow beans, fresh	500 ml	(2 cups)
Green beans, fresh	500 ml	(2 cups)
Carrots, in round slices	2	
Beef broth or other flavor	250 ml	(1 cup)
Thyme, fresh, oregano, basil	a pinch of each	
Pepper, salt or no-salt shaker (pg. 155)	to taste	
Rosemary	a pinch	

1. In a pot, cook the ground meat with onion and celery,
   without added fat, for 10 minutes.
2. Moisten with some broth or water as needed.
3. Add the 8 other ingredients.
4. Cover and cook over medium heat for approx. 20 minutes.
5. Serve.

One portion equals:
3 meats + 3 vegetables + 1 bread.

319 kilocalories   32 g proteins   36 g carbohydrates   6 g fat
43 mg cholesterol   9 g fiber   8 mg iron   127 mg calcium
103 mg magnesium   1671 mg potassium   318 mg sodium

Pepper Steak

Preparation time: 2 hours   Cooking time: 10 minutes
4 servings

Lemon juice	15 ml	(1 tbsp.)
Worcestershire sauce	5 ml	(1 tsp.)
Parsley, fresh, chopped	5 ml	(1 tsp.)
Garlic powder	1 ml	(1/4 tsp.)
Olive oil, canola oil or other	5 ml	(1 tsp.)
Pepper in corns, ground	to taste	
Steak of your choice (4 slices)	454 g	(1 pound)

1. Mix the first 6 ingredients in a pan.
2. Spread the mixture on both sides of each steak.
3. Let marinate for approx. 2 hours.
4. Cook the steaks on each side as desired, without added fat.
5. Serve with baked potatoes or rice, and an attractive salad.

One portion equals:
3 meats.

193 kilocalories   27 g proteins   1 g carbohydrate   9 g fat
54 mg cholesterol   0 g fiber   2 mg iron   7 mg calcium
27 mg magnesium   550 mg potassium   77 mg sodium

44

Beef with Broccoli and Clementines

Preparation time: 10 minutes   Cooking time: 30 minutes
4 servings

Beef, tender, strips	454 g	(1 pound)
Onion, in round slices	1	
Garlic, minced	1 clove	
Celery, cut on a diagonal	1 stalk	
Milk (2% m.f. or less)	60 ml	(1/4 cup)
Chicken broth, defatted	250 ml	(1 cup)
Flour of your choice	15 ml	(1 tbsp.)
Ginger, fresh, chopped	30 ml	(2 tbsps.)
Red pepper, in strips	1	
Broccoli, raw, in florets	500 ml	(2 cups)
Cauliflower, in florets	500 ml	(2 cups)
Clementines, in quarters	4	

1. Cook the first 4 ingredients in a pot with no added fat for approx. 10 minutes.
2. Moisten with some broth or water as needed.
3. Mix the next 8 ingredients in a bowl.
5. Cover and continue cooking over medium heat for approx. 8 minutes.
6. Serve.

One portion equals:
3 meats + 2 vegetables + 1/2 fruit.

276 kilocalories   30 g proteins   26 g carbohydrates   7 g fat
44 mg cholesterol   4 g fiber   3 mg iron   94 mg calcium
70 mg magnesium   1140 mg potassium   306 mg sodium

45

Meatloaf Feast

Preparation time: 10 minutes   Cooking time: 60 minutes
4 servings

Beef or veal, lean ground	454 g	(1 pound)
Onion, minced	1	
Oatmeal, raw (oat flakes)	60 ml	(1/4 cup)
Carrots, grated	2	
Celery, chopped	1 stalk	
Oregano, fresh, thyme, basil	a pinch of each	
Pepper, salt or no-salt shaker (pg. 155)	to taste	
Egg, beaten	1	
Cheese (20% m.f. or less), grated	60 ml	(1/4 cup)
Tomato juice	125 ml	(1/2 cup)

1. Mix the first 8 ingredients.
2. Add to a greased bread pan.
3. Bake uncovered in the oven at 180ºC (350ºF) for approx. 50 minutes.
4. Add the cheese and the tomato juice.
5. Continue cooking for 10 minutes.
6. Cool for 5 minutes and slice.
7. Serve.

One portion equals:
3 meats + 1 vegetable + 1/2 milk.

277 kilocalories   32 g proteins   14 g carbohydrates   10 g fat
10 mg cholesterol   3 g fiber   2 mg iron   149 mg calcium
52 mg magnesium   816 mg potassium   283 mg sodium

Sausage with Vegetables

Preparation time: 15 minutes   Cooking time: 15 minutes
4 servings

Sausages, low fat (tofu, beef, turkey...)	8 sausages	
Onion, minced	1	
Carrot, cubed	1	
Green pepper, in strips	1	
Celery, cubed	2 stalks	
Mushrooms, sliced	125 ml	(1/2 cup)
Garlic, minced	1 clove	
Ketchup	45 ml	(3 tbsps.)
Soy sauce	15 ml	(1 tbsp.)
Chicken broth, defatted or other	250 ml	(1 cup)

1. Cook the sausages in boiling water in a saucepan for approx. 5 minutes.
2. Strain.
3. In a large pan, brown the sausages with onion, without added fat, over low heat.
4. Add some broth as needed.
5. Mix the 8 other ingredients and put in a bowl.
6. Cover the sausages with these ingredients.
7. Bake uncovered for approx. 10 minutes or until the vegetables are cooked to your taste.
8. Serve.

One portion equals:
2 meats + 2 vegetables + 1 fat.

231 kilocalories   13 g proteins   15 g carbohydrates   14 g fat
80 mg cholesterol   2 g fiber   2 mg iron   114 mg calcium
29 mg magnesium   532 mg potassium   1648 mg sodium

Meat Similipizza

Preparation time: 10 minutes   Cooking time: 35 minutes
6 servings

Beef or veal, lean ground	454 g	(1 pound)
Basil, fresh	15 ml	(1 tbsp.)
Pepper	to taste	
Onion powder and garlic powder	a pinch of each	
Breadcrumbs	250 ml	(1 cup)
Egg, beaten	1	
Onion, minced	1	
Pizza sauce or tomato sauce	125 ml	(1/2 cup)
Mushrooms, fresh, sliced	250 ml	(1 cup)
Red pepper, in strips	1	
Green pepper, in strips	1	
Cheese (20% m.f. or less), grated	250 ml	(1 cup)

1. Mix the first 7 ingredients.
2. Put and press this mixture into the base of a square pan for the oven.
3. Spread the sauce on top of the mixture.
4. Top with mushrooms and strips of peppers.
5. Sprinkle with grated cheese.
6. Bake uncovered in the oven at 180°C (350°F) for approx. 30-40 minutes.

One portion equals:
3 meats + 1 vegetable + 1/2 bread + 1 milk.

360 kilocalories   34 g proteins   25 g carbohydrates   14 g fat
89 mg cholesterol   3 g fiber   3 mg iron   406 mg calcium
53 mg magnesium   699 mg potassium   605 mg sodium

Cabbage Cigars

Preparation time: 20 minutes   Cooking time: 60 minutes
4 servings

Beef or veal, lean ground	454 g	(1 pound)
Onion, minced	1	
Green pepper, minced	1	
Breadcrumbs	60 ml	(1/4 cup)
Egg, beaten	1	
Basil, fresh	30 ml	(2 tbsps.)
Pepper, salt or no-salt shaker (pg. 155)	to taste	
Cabbage leaves, blanched	8	
Tomato juice	500 ml	(2 cups)

1. Mix the first 7 ingredients.
2. Divide into 8 portions.
3. Put the mix on the cabbage leaves and roll to make cigars.
4. Prick with a large toothpick.
5. Put the cigars in a pan for the oven.
6. Add the tomato juice.
7. Cover and cook in the oven at 180ºC (350ºF) for approx. 60 minutes.
8. Serve.

One portion of 2 cigars equals:
3 meats + 2 vegetables.

248 kilocalories   28 g proteins   18 g carbohydrates   7 g fat
97 mg cholesterol   2 g fiber   3 mg iron   45 mg calcium
52 mg magnesium   960 mg potassium   741 mg sodium

49

Shepherd's Pie Surprise

Preparation time: 20 minutes   Cooking time: 30 minutes
6 servings

Beef or veal, lean ground	454 g	(1 pound)
Onion, minced	1 medium	
Pepper, salt or no-salt shaker (pg. 155)	to taste	
Onion powder and garlic powder	a pinch of each	
Lentils, cooked, drained	540 ml	(1 x 19 oz can)
Corn, creamed or kernel	284 ml	(1 x 10 oz can)
Potatoes, cooked	4	
Milk (2% m.f. or less)	125 ml	(1/2 cup)
Pepper, salt, onion powder	to taste	
Paprika	a pinch	

1. Cook the first 4 ingredients in a frying pan without added fat.
2. Put in a square baking pan for the oven. Season.
3. Add the lentils and the corn on top of the meat.
4. Purée the vegetables, adding the milk, pepper, salt, and onion powder.
5. Put the purée on top and sprinkle with paprika.
6. Bake in the oven uncovered at 180ºC (350ºF) for approx. 30 minutes.
7. Serve.

One portion equals:
2 meats + 2 vegetables + 2 breads.

306 kilocalories   26 g proteins   42 g carbohydrates   5 g fat
30 mg cholesterol   5 g fiber   4 mg iron   57 mg calcium
73 mg magnesium   1160 mg potassium   201 mg sodium

Chop Suey

Preparation time: 10 minutes   Cooking time: 30 minutes
4 servings

Beef or veal, lean ground	454 g	(1 pound)
Onion, minced	1	
Celery, chopped	2 stalks	
Broth of your choice	250 ml	(1 cup)
Flour of your choice	15 ml	(1 tbsp.)
Soy sauce	30 ml	(2 tbsps.)
Mushrooms, sliced	250 ml	(1 cup)
Beansprouts, raw	500 ml	(2 cups)
Pepper	to taste	

1. Cook the first 3 ingredients in a pot over medium heat without added fat.
2. Moisten with some broth or water as needed.
3. Mix the 6 other ingredients and put in the pot. Continue cooking for approx. 20 minutes.
4. Cover and continue cooking over medium heat for approx. 15 minutes.
5. Serve.

One portion equals:
4 meats + 2 vegetables.

235 kilocalories   31 g proteins   11 g carbohydrates   8 g fat
43 mg cholesterol   1 g fiber   3 mg iron   52 mg calcium
61 mg magnesium   915 mg potassium   706 mg sodium

Meat Pie

Preparation time: 20 minutes   Cooking time: 45 minutes
6 servings

Beef or veal, lean ground . . . . 227 g   (1/2 pound)
Pork, lean ground . . . . 227 g   (1/2 pound)
Onion, minced 1
Onion powder and garlic powder . . . . a pinch of each
Cloves, ground . . . . 1/2 ml   (1/4 tsp.)
Cinnamon . . . . 1/2 ml   (1/4 tsp.)
Nutmeg . . . . 1/2 ml   (1/4 tsp.)
Pepper, salt or no-salt shaker (pg. 155) . . . . . . to taste

HEALTHY PIE CRUST
Flour, whole wheat . . . . 500 ml   (2 cups)
Oil, non hydrogenated margarine, or butter . . . . 60 ml   (1/4 cup)
Yogurt, plain (2% m.f. or less) . . . . 180 ml   (3/4 cup)
Water . . . . 30 ml   (2 tbsps.)

1. Cook the meat with onion and seasonings but without added fat
   for approx. 20 minutes.
2. Put in an uncooked pie shell. Prepare the pastry following the instructions
   on pg. 142.
3. Cover with the pastry lid and seal at the edge of the pie plate.
4. Make small incisions in the top of the pastry.
5. Bake in the oven at 210ºC (425ºF) for approx. 20-25 minutes.
6. Serve.

One portion equals:
3 meats + 1 fat + 2 breads.

348 kilocalories   24 g proteins   36 g carbohydrates   13 g fat
36 mg cholesterol   6 g fiber   3 mg iron   77 mg calcium
84 mg magnesium   590 mg potassium   62 mg sodium

Dijon Veal or Beef

Preparation time: 15 minutes   Cooking time: 15 minutes
4 servings

Beef or veal, lean, in strips	454 g	(1 pound)
White wine	30 ml	(2 tbsps.)
Shallots, thin slices	2	
Dijon mustard	60 ml	(1/4 cup)
Red wine or white	250 ml	(1 cup)
Milk (2% m.f. or less)	250 ml	(1 cup)
Flour of your choice	30 ml	(2 tbsps.)
Coriander, ground	2 ml	(1/2 tsp.)
Pepper, salt or no-salt shaker (pg. 155)	to taste	

1. Cook the veal or beef with shallots and wine, with no added fat, in a pan for approx. 10 minutes.
2. Mix the 6 other ingredients without making lumps.
3. Add this mixture to the meat.
4. Stir until thickened.
5. Serve with rice, rice vermicelli or plain potato, mashed potato, or healthy fries (pg. 77).

One portion equals:
3 meats + 1/2 bread + 1/2 milk.

295 kilocalories   29 g proteins   11 g carbohydrates   10 g fat
48 mg cholesterol   1 g fiber   3 mg iron   143 mg calcium
73 mg magnesium   745 mg potassium   93 mg sodium

Meatloaf Surprise

Preparation time: 15 minutes   Cooking time: 60 minutes
4 servings

Beef or veal, lean ground	454 g	(1 pound)
Onion, minced	1	
Oatmeal, raw	125 ml	(1/2 cup)
Green pepper, diced	1/2	
Celery, chopped	1 stalk	
Basil, fresh	30 ml	(2 tbsps.)
Pepper, salt or no-salt shaker (pg. 155)	to taste	
Cream of celery soup	284 ml	(1 x 10 oz can)
Spinach, raw, chopped	250 ml	(1 cup)
Cheese (20% m.f. or less), grated	125 ml	(1/2 cup)

1. Mix the first 8 ingredients.
2. Put one third of the mixture in a bread pan.
3. Layer a row of spinach alternately with a row of meat.
4. Bake uncovered in the oven at 180°C (350°F) for approx. 60 minutes.
5. Add the cheese and grill for 3 minutes.
6. Serve with a tomato sauce (pg.34).

One portion equals:
3 meats + 1 vegetable + 1 milk.

352 kilocalories   37 g proteins   19 g carbohydrates   14 g fat
66 mg cholesterol   3 g fiber   3 mg iron   306 mg calcium
75 mg magnesium   835 mg potassium   545 mg sodium

Meatballs with Rice

Preparation time: 20 minutes   Cooking time: 30 minutes
4 servings

Beef or veal, lean ground	454 g	(1 pound)
Brown rice, long grain, uncooked	60 ml	(1/4 cup)
Onion powder, garlic powder, and nutmeg	a pinch of each	
Pepper	a pinch	
Celery, cut on a diagonal	1 stalk	
Carrots, cubed	2	
Tomato juice	1.36 L	(1 x 48 oz can)
Onion, minced	1	
Sugar, brown or white	15 ml	(1 tbsp.)
Basil, fresh	5 ml	(1 tsp.)
Herbs	5 ml	(1 tsp.)
Onion powder, garlic powder, and nutmeg	a pinch of each	
Pepper, salt or no-salt shaker (pg. 155)	to taste	

1. Mix the first 4 ingredients.
2. Form this meat mixture into 20 meatballs (5 per portion).
3. Mix the 9 other ingredients and bring to a boil in a pot.
4. Add the meatballs gently to the boiling liquid.
5. Cook uncovered over medium heat for approx. 30 minutes.
6. Serve with rice, pasta, or mashed potato.

One portion equals:
3 meats + 2 vegetables + 1/2 bread.

242 kilocalories   26 g proteins   20 g carbohydrates   6 g fat
43 mg cholesterol   2 g fiber   2 mg iron   33 mg calcium
52 mg magnesium   749 mg potassium   81 mg sodium

Beef or Veal Stroganoff

Preparation time: 15 minutes   Cooking time: 10 minutes
4 servings

Beef or veal, lean, in strips	454 g	(1 pound)
Onion, chopped	1	
Mushrooms, sliced	250 ml	(1 cup)
Carrot, in thin round slices	1	
Red wine	60 ml	(1/4 cup)
Onion powder and garlic powder	a pinch of each	
Beef broth, powder or cubes	5 ml	(1 tsp.)
Pepper, salt or no-salt shaker (pg. 155)	to taste	
Sour cream (14% m.f.) or plain yogurt	15 ml	(1 tbsp.)
Parmesan cheese (20% m.f. or less), grated . .	30 ml	(2 tbsps.)
Milk (2% m.f. or less)	250 ml	(1 cup)
Flour of your choice	30 ml	(2 tbsps.)

1. In a pot, cook the meat strips with onion, mushrooms, and carrot for approx. 10 minutes.
2. Moisten with some broth or water as needed.
3. Mix the 8 other ingredients without making lumps.
4. Add to the meat and vegetable mixture and continue cooking until it thickens.
5. Serve with pasta, rice, or potato.

One portion equals:
3 meats + 2 vegetables + 1 fat.

244 kilocalories   28 g proteins   13 g carbohydrates   7 g fat
49 mg cholesterol   2 g fiber   2 mg iron   105 mg calcium
45 mg magnesium   822 mg potassium   104 mg sodium

Fruity Chicken

Preparation time: 15 minutes   Cooking time: 50 minutes
4 servings

Breadcrumbs	80 ml	(1/3 cup)
Tarragon	5 ml	(1 tsp.)
Paprika	5 ml	(1 tsp.)
Nutmeg	1 ml	(1/4 tsp.)
Pepper, salt or no-salt shaker (pg. 155)	to taste	
Chicken breasts, boneless (4 breasts)	454 g	(1 pound)
Orange juice or apple juice or wine	125 ml	(1/2 cup)
Broth of your choice	125 ml	(1/2 cup)
Shallot, minced	1	
Peaches or mandarins, in pieces	250 ml	(1 cup)
Flour of your choice	15 ml	(1 tbsp.)
Pepper, salt or no-salt shaker (pg. 155)	to taste	

1. Mix the first 5 other ingredients (seasoned breadcrumbs).
2. Cover the chicken breasts with seasoned breadcrumbs.
3. Put in a greased rectangular baking pan for the oven.
4. Bake in the oven at 180ºC (350ºF) for approx. 35 minutes.
5. Mix the 6 other ingredients.
6. Add this mixture onto the chicken.
7. Continue cooking uncovered for approx. 15 minutes.

One portion equals:
3 meats + 1/2 bread + 1/2 fruit.

194 kilocalories   21 g proteins   19 g carbohydrates   3 g fat
49 mg cholesterol   2 g fiber   2 mg iron   46 mg calcium
30 mg magnesium   362 mg potassium   233 mg sodium

Seafood-Filled Crêpes

Preparation time: 20 minutes   Cooking time: 20 minutes
4 servings

CRÊPES
Flour, whole wheat	250 ml	(1 cup)
Milk (2% m.f. or less)	250 ml	(1 cup)
Egg, beaten	1	
Salt	a pinch	

WHITE SAUCE
Milk (2% m.f. or less)	250 ml	(1 cup)
Flour, whole wheat	60 ml	(1/4 cup)
Onion powder and garlic powder	to taste	
Pepper, salt or no-salt shaker (pg. 155)	to taste	

TOPPING
Shrimp, cooked	16 small
Scallops, cooked	16 small
Asparagus, cooked	8 spears

Cheese (20% m.f. or less), grated	125 ml	(1/2 cup)

1. Mix the first 4 ingredients (crêpe batter).
2. Cook 4 small crêpes in a non-stick frying pan.
3. Let cool. Mix the white sauce ingredients.
4. Cook until thickened and lower the heat.
5. Stuff each crêpe with 4 shrimps, 4 scallops, 2 spears of asparagus and some white sauce.
6. Roll each stuffed crêpe. Put in a greased pan for the oven.
7. Pour the remaining sauce onto the crêpes. Top with grated cheese.
8. Broil in the oven for approx. 5-10 minutes. Serve.

One portion equals:
2 meats + 1 1/2 breads + 1 milk.

340 kilocalories   25 g proteins   38 g carbohydrates   11 g fat
90 mg cholesterol   5 g fiber   2 mg iron   439 mg calcium
99 mg magnesium   531 mg potassium   305 mg sodium

Chicken Chow Mein

Preparation time: 15 minutes   Cooking time: 20 minutes
4 servings

Chicken, uncooked, in strips	454 g	(1 pound)
Onion, minced	1	
Garlic, minced	1 clove	
Celery, cut on a diagonal	1 stalk	
Carrot, in round slices	1	
Soy sauce	45 ml	(3 tbsps.)
Mushrooms, whole	250 ml	(1 cup)
Green pepper, in pieces	1	
Tarragon	1 ml	(1/4 tsp.)
Chinese cabbage, in pieces	500 ml	(2 cups)
Chicken broth, defatted	250 ml	(1 cup)
Cornstarch	30 ml	(2 tbsps.)
Water	60 ml	(1/4 cup)
Pepper, salt or no-salt shaker (pg. 155)	to taste	

1. Cook the first 5 ingredients in a pot over medium heat without added fat for approx. 10 minutes.
2. Moisten with some broth or water as needed.
3. Mix the 9 other ingredients and put in the pot.
4. Cover and continue cooking over low heat for approx. 15 minutes.
5. Serve.

One portion equals:
3 meats + 2 vegetables.

175 kilocalories   22 g proteins   15 g carbohydrates   3 g fat
49 mg cholesterol   3 g fiber   2 mg iron   77 mg calcium
38 mg magnesium   570 mg potassium   919 mg sodium

Hunter's Chicken

Preparation time: 20 minutes   Cooking time: 50 minutes
4 servings

Chicken breasts, boneless	454 g	(1 pound)
Onion, minced	1	
Celery, cut on a diagonal	2 stalks	
Mushrooms, sliced	500 ml	(2 cups)
Garlic, minced	1 clove	
Cloves, ground	a pinch	
Bay leaves	1	
Pepper, salt or no-salt shaker (pg. 155)	to taste	
Tomatoes, canned, crushed	540 ml	(1 x 19 oz can)
Green olives, small (optional)	125 ml	(1/2 cup)

1. Cook the first 5 ingredients in a pot over medium heat without added fat for approx. 10 minutes.
2. Moisten with some broth or water as needed.
3. Mix the 5 other ingredients and put in the pot.
4. Cover and continue cooking over low heat for approx. 40 minutes.
5. Serve with pasta, rice, or other.

One portion equals:
3 meats + 2 vegetables.

194 kilocalories   21 g proteins   14 g carbohydrates   7 g fat
49 mg cholesterol   4 g fiber   3 mg iron   62 mg calcium
40 mg magnesium   665 mg potassium   346 mg sodium

Breaded Honey Chicken

Preparation time: 5 minutes   Cooking time: 45 minutes
4 servings

Breadcrumbs	125 ml	(1/2 cup)
Cake flour	30 ml	(2 tbsps.)
Tarragon	2 ml	(1/2 tsp.)
Thyme, fresh	5 ml	(1 tsp.)
Basil, fresh	15 ml	(1 tbsp.)
Paprika	2 ml	(1/2 tsp.)
Chicken breasts, boneless	454 g	(1 pound)

HONEY SAUCE

Honey	30 ml	(2 tbsps.)
Chicken broth, defatted	250 ml	(1 cup)
Flour of your choice	15 ml	(1 tbsp.)
Parsley, fresh, pepper and salt	a pinch of each	

1. Mix the first 5 ingredients (seasoned breadcrumbs).
2. Cover the chicken breasts with seasoned breadcrumbs.
3. Put the chicken breasts on a greased cookie sheet.
4. Bake the chicken uncovered in the oven at 180ºC (350ºF) for approx. 35-45 minutes.
5. Mix the sauce ingredients in a small saucepan.
6. Cook this mixture for approx. 7 minutes until thickened.
7. Serve the chicken with honey sauce.

One portion equals:
3 meats + 1/2 bread + 1 fruit.

222 kilocalories   22 g proteins   25 g carbohydrates   4 g fat
49 mg cholesterol   1 g fiber   2 mg iron   53 mg calcium
25 mg magnesium   208 mg potassium   385 mg sodium

Chicken Squares

Preparation time: 15 minutes   Cooking time: 30 minutes
8 servings

Chicken, in pieces	500 ml	(2 cups)
Breadcrumbs	60 ml	(1/4 cup)
Oatmeal, raw	60 ml	(1/4 cup)
Celery, chopped	1 stalk	
Carrot, grated	1	
Green pepper, minced	1	
Onion, minced	1	
Garlic, minced	1 clove	
Eggs, beaten	2	
Chicken broth, defatted	250 ml	(1 cup)
Milk (2% m.f. or less)	125 ml	(1/2 cup)
Pepper, salt or no-salt shaker (pg. 155)	to taste	
Cheese (20% m.f. or less), grated	250 ml	(1 cup)

1. Mix all ingredients.
2. Put in a greased square baking pan for the oven.
3. Bake uncovered in the oven at 180ºC (350ºF) for approx. 30 minutes.
4. Serve with a white sauce (pg. 34).

One portion equals:
3 meats + 1 vegetable + 1/2 milk.

242 kilocalories   28 g proteins   9 g carbohydrates   10 g fat
15 mg cholesterol   1 g fiber   1 mg iron   299 mg calcium
36 mg magnesium   318 mg potassium   353 mg sodium

Chicken Stew

Preparation time: 15 minutes   Cooking time: 40 minutes
4 servings

Chicken, cubed	454 g	(1 pound)
Onion, minced	1	
Carrot, in round slices	1	
Chicken broth, defatted	125 ml	(1/2 cup)
Cabbage, in pieces	250 ml	(1 cup)
Celery, in pieces	1 stalk	
Rutabaga, cubed	125 ml	(1/2 cup)
Potatoes, in pieces	4	
Chicken broth, defatted	250 ml	(1 cup)
Onion powder and garlic powder	a pinch of each	
Flour of your choice	15 ml	(1 tbsp.)
Tarragon	2 ml	(1/2 tsp.)
Pepper, salt or no-salt shaker (pg. 155)	to taste	

1. Cook the first 4 ingredients in a pot over medium heat without added fat for approx. 10 minutes.
2. Add the 9 other ingredients to the pot.
3. Cover and continue cooking over low heat for approx. 30 minutes.
4. Serve.

One portion equals:
3 meats + 2 vegetables + 1 bread.

241 kilocalories   23 g proteins   30 g carbohydrates   3 g fat
49 mg cholesterol   4 g fiber   2 mg iron   56 mg calcium
54 mg magnesium   1024 mg potassium   390 mg sodium

Sunny Chicken

Preparation time: 15 minutes   Cooking time: 20 minutes
4 servings

Chicken, cubed . . . . 454 g   (1 pound)
Onion, minced 1
Garlic, minced . . . . 1 clove
Carrots, in thin round slices 2
Celery, minced . . . . 2 stalks

Broccoli, raw, in florets . . . . 500 ml   (2 cups)
Mushrooms, sliced . . . . 250 ml   (1 cup)
Chicken broth, defatted . . . . 125 ml   (1/2 cup)
Fruit juice (orange, pineapple, etc.) . . . . 125 ml   (1/2 cup)
Flour of your choice . . . . 15 ml   (1 tbsp.)
Ginger, ground . . . . a pinch
Rosemary . . . . a pinch
Pepper, salt or no-salt shaker (pg. 155) . . . . . . a pinch

1. Cook the first 5 ingredients in a pot over medium heat without added fat
   for approx. 10 minutes.
2. Moisten with some broth or water as needed.
3. Mix the 8 other ingredients and put in the pot.
4. Cover and continue cooking over medium heat for approx. 10 minutes.
5. Serve.

One portion equals:
3 meats + 2 vegetables.

183 kilocalories   22 g proteins   18 g carbohydrates   3 g fat
49 mg cholesterol   3 g fiber   2 mg iron   65 mg calcium
43 mg magnesium   640 mg potassium   193 mg sodium

B.B.Q. Chicken

Preparation time: 10 minutes   Cooking time: 25 minutes
4 servings

Chicken breasts, boneless	454 g	(1 pound)
Onion, chopped	1	
Garlic, minced	1 clove	
Chicken broth, defatted	125 ml	(1/2 cup)
Ketchup	125 ml	(1/2 cup)
Worcestershire sauce	2 ml	(1/2 tsp.)
Soy sauce	15 ml	(1 tbsp.)
Mustard, dried	2 ml	(1/2 tsp.)
Lemon juice	30 ml	(2 tbsps.)
Onion powder	2 ml	(1/2 tsp.)
Garlic powder	1 ml	(1/4 tsp.)

Pepper, salt or no-salt shaker (pg. 155) . . . . . . to taste

1. Cook the first 3 ingredients in a pot over medium heat without added fat for approx. 10 minutes.
2. Moisten with some broth or water as needed.
3. Mix the 9 other ingredients in a small bowl.
4. Incorporate this mixture to the chicken.
5. Continue cooking uncovered over medium heat for approx. 10 minutes.
6. Serve with healthy fries (pg. 77) and with an attractive salad.

One portion equals:
3 meats + 1 vegetable + 1/2 bread.

161 kilocalories   20 g proteins   14 g carbohydrates   3 g fat
49 mg cholesterol   1 g fiber   1 mg iron   30 mg calcium
29 mg magnesium   381 mg potassium   737 mg sodium

Thai Turkey or Chicken

Preparation time: 10 minutes   Cooking time: 20 minutes
4 servings

Turkey or chicken, uncooked, in strips	454 g	(1 pound)
Onion, minced	1	
Chicken broth, defatted	125 ml	(1/2 cup)
Lemon or orange zest	30 ml	(2 tbsps.)
Lemon juice	80 ml	(1/3 cup)
Oyster sauce	60 ml	(1/4 cup)
Ketchup	30 ml	(2 tbsps.)
Teriyaki sauce	30 ml	(2 tbsps.)
Pepper flakes, ground	1 ml	(1/4 tsp.)
Garlic, chopped	1 clove	
Snow peas, cooked	250 ml	(1 cup)
Tomato, diced	1	

1. Cook the first 2 ingredients in a pot over medium heat without added fat for approx. 10 minutes.
2. Moisten with some broth or water as needed.
3. Mix the 10 other ingredients and add the poultry.
4. Cover and continue cooking for approx. 10 minutes.
5. Serve with rice vermicelli or plain rice.
6. Serve with an attractive salad.

One portion equals:
3 meats + 1 vegetable + 1/2 bread.

153 kilocalories   20 g proteins   15 g carbohydrates   2 g fat
55 mg cholesterol   3 g fiber   3 mg iron   52 mg calcium
48 mg magnesium   566 mg potassium   976 mg sodium

Meat Brochette

Preparation time: 6 hours   Cooking time: 15-40 minutes
4 servings

Beef or veal, cubed	454 g	(1 pound)
Olive oil, canola oil or other	60 ml	(1/4 cup)
Lemon juice or vinegar	60 ml	(1/4 cup)
Orange juice	30 ml	(2 tbsps.)
Garlic, minced	1 clove	
Oregano, fresh, thyme and garlic powder	a pinch of each	
Parsley, fresh, chopped	5 ml	(1 tsp.)
Pepper, salt or no-salt shaker (pg. 155)	to taste	
Mushroom tops	8	
Green pepper	8 pieces	
Onion	8 pieces	
Tomatoes, cubed	8	

1. Mix the first 8 ingredients (marinade).
2. Let marinate for approx. 6 hours.
3. Strain the mixture.
4. Skewer the cubes of meat alternating with vegetables.
5. Bake in the oven at 180ºC (350ºF) for approx. 15 to 40 minutes.
6. Spread with marinade while cooking.
7. Serve with rice and salad.

One portion equals:
3 meats + 2 vegetables.

334 kilocalories   21 g proteins   19 g carbohydrates   20 g fat
39 mg cholesterol   4 g fiber   3 mg iron   33 mg calcium
56 mg magnesium   1165 mg potassium   74 mg sodium

Chili Con Carne

Preparation time: 10 minutes   Cooking time: 30 minutes
6 servings

Beef or veal, lean ground	454 g	(1 pound)
Onion, minced	1	
Garlic, minced	1 clove	
Celery, chopped	1 stalk	
Tomato juice	125 ml	(1/2 cup)
Green pepper, in small pieces	1	
Red pepper, in small pieces	1	
Tomatoes, in pieces	540 ml	(1 x 19 oz can)
Chili powder	10 ml	(2 tsps.)
Oregano, fresh	15 ml	(1 tbsp.)
Basil, fresh	30 ml	(2 tbsps.)
Red kidney beans, cooked, drained and rinsed .	540 ml	(1 x 19 oz can)

1. Cook the first 4 ingredients in a pot over medium heat without added fat for approx. 10 minutes.
2. Moisten with some broth or water as needed.
3. Add the 7 other ingredients (except the beans) to the pot.
4. Cover and continue cooking for approx. 20 minutes over medium heat.
5. Add the cooked red kidney beans.
6. Cover and continue cooking for approx. 5 extra minutes.
7. Add the tomato juice or water if the texture is too thick.
8. Serve with rice or pasta.

One portion equals:
3 meats + 2 vegetables + 1 bread.

241 kilocalories   24 g proteins   28 g carbohydrates   5 g fat
29 mg cholesterol   3 g fiber   4 mg iron   59 mg calcium
71 mg magnesium   1032 mg potassium   141 mg sodium

Vegetarian Spaghetti Sauce

Preparation time: 15 minutes   Cooking time: 60 minutes
4 servings

Tofu, firm, cubed or crumbled	454 g	(1 pound)
Tomatoes, in pieces	540 ml	(1 x 19 oz can)
Tomato paste	156 ml	(1 x 5 1/2 oz can)
Water	250 ml	(1 cup)
Carrot, grated	1	
Mushrooms, sliced	250 ml	(1 cup)
Green pepper, in pieces	1	
Onion, minced	1	
Garlic powder, thyme, oregano, basil . . .	a pinch of each	
Cayenne pepper	1 ml	(1/4 tsp.)
Pepper, salt or no-salt shaker (pg. 155) .	to taste	

1. Mix all ingredients in a pot.
2. Cover and cook over low heat for approx. 60 minutes.
3. Serve with pasta, rice, couscous, or cooked spaghetti squash.

One portion equals:
2 meats + 3 vegetables + 1/2 milk.

269 kilocalories   22 g proteins   28 g carbohydrates   11 g fat
0 mg cholesterol   6 g fiber   14 mg iron   273 mg calcium
156 mg magnesium   1229 mg potassium   65 mg sodium

Veggie-Pâté

Sunflower seeds	250 ml	(1 cup)
Flour, whole wheat	125 ml	(1/2 cup)
Potato, raw and grated	1	
Onion, minced	1	
Lemon juice	15 ml	(1 tbsp.)
Olive oil, canola oil or other	20 ml	(4 tsps.)
Chicken broth, defatted or other	375 ml	(1 1/2 cups)
Thyme, fresh, basil, sage	a pinch of each	
Pepper, salt or no-salt shaker (pg. 155) . . .	to taste	

1. Mix all ingredients in a food processor.
2. Put in a greased square baking pan.
3. Bake in the oven at 180°C (350°F) for approx. 50 minutes.
4. Serve cold as a spread.

One portion equals:
1 meat + 2 fat + 1 bread.

180 kilocalories   5 g proteins   14 g carbohydrates   13 g fat
0 mg cholesterol   2 g fiber   2 mg iron   26 mg calcium
42 mg magnesium   263 mg potassium   159 mg sodium

Legume-Loaf

Chickpeas, cooked	540 ml	(1 x 19 oz can)
Onion, minced	1	
Celery, chopped	1 stalk	
Egg, beaten	1	
Oatmeal, raw	60 ml	(1/4 cup)
Garlic powder	1 ml	(1/4 tsp.)
Parsley, fresh, chopped	5 ml	(1 tsp.)
Basil, fresh	2 ml	(1/2 tsp.)
Worcestershire sauce	2 ml	(1/2 tsp.)
Pepper, salt or no-salt shaker (pg. 155)	to taste	
Cheese (20% m.f. or less), grated	250 ml	(1 cup)

1. Purée all ingredients in a food processor.
2. Add to a greased bread pan.
3. Bake in the oven at 180ºC (350ºF) for approx. 45 minutes.
4. Let cool before cutting.
5. Serve plain or with tomato sauce.

One portion equals:
1 meat + 2 vegetables + 1 milk.

272 kilocalories   20 g proteins   24 g carbohydrates   11 g fat
61 mg cholesterol   4 g fiber   2 mg iron   381 mg calcium
53 mg magnesium   321 mg potassium   267 mg sodium

Baked Beans Without Lard

Preparation time: 15 minutes   Cooking time: 6 hours
8 servings

White beans, uncooked	500 ml	(2 cups)
Water for soaking	to cover beans	
Water for cooking	1 L	(4 cups)
Molasses	60 ml	(1/4 cup)
Mustard, dried	2 ml	(1/2 tsp.)
Onion, minced	1	
Ketchup	60 ml	(1/4 cup)

1. Cover the beans with water and let soak over night.
2. Strain the beans and throw away the soaking water.
3. Put in a bean casserole dish.
4. Mix the 5 other ingredients and add to the beans.
5. Cover and cook in the oven at 120°C (250°F) for approx. 5 hours.
6. Uncover and continue cooking for 1 hour.
7. Add water as needed.
8. Serve.

One portion equals:
1 meat + 1 vegetable + 2 breads + 1/2 milk.

223 kilocalories   13 g proteins   43 g carbohydrates   1 g fat
0 mg cholesterol   8 g fiber   6 mg iron   156 mg calcium
131 mg magnesium   1183 mg potassium   103 mg sodium

72

Chinese Tofu

Preparation time: 10 minutes   Cooking time: 15 minutes
4 servings

Tofu, firm, in pieces or strips	454 g	(1 pound)
Onion, in round slices	1	
Carrot, in thin sticks	1	
Celery, cut on a diagonal	2 stalks	
Soy sauce	60 ml	(1/4 cup)
Broth of your choice	60 ml	(1/4 cup)
Cauliflower, in florets	250 ml	(1 cup)
Broth of your choice	250 ml	(1 cup)
Flour of your choice	15 ml	(1 tbsp.)
Green pepper, in strips	1	
Red pepper, in strips	1	
Pepper	to taste	
Ginger, ground	a pinch	
Onion powder and garlic powder	a pinch of each	

1. Cook the first 7 ingredients in a saucepan with no added fat for approx. 10 minutes.
2. Mix the other ingredients in a large bowl without making lumps.
3. Add to the tofu mixture.
4. Continue cooking uncovered over medium heat for approx. 5 minutes until vegetables are tender.
5. Add the soy sauce as needed.
6. Serve as is or over rice.

One portion equals:
2 1/2 meats + 2 vegetables + 1/2 milk.

242 kilocalories   22 g proteins   21 g carbohydrates   11 g fat
0 mg cholesterol   4 g fiber   13 mg iron   274 mg calcium
130 mg magnesium   721 mg potassium   1141 mg sodium

Vegetarian Hamburger

Preparation time: 15 minutes   Cooking time: 10 minutes
6 servings

Tofu, firm, finely crumbled	454 g	(1 pound)
Onion, finely chopped	1	
Red pepper, chopped	30 ml	(2 tbsps.)
Egg, beaten	1	
Flour, whole wheat	30 ml	(2 tbsps.)
Oatmeal, raw	250 ml	(1 cup)
Sunflower seeds, chopped	30 ml	(2 tbsps.)
Soy sauce	15 ml	(1 tbsp.)
Thyme, fresh, basil, oregano	a pinch of each	
Pepper, salt or no-salt shaker (pg. 155)	to taste	
Hamburger buns, whole wheat	4	

1. Mix all ingredients.
2. Form into 4 patties.
3. Cook in a lightly greased frying pan for approx. 10 minutes.
4. Serve plain, with your choice of sauce, or on a hamburger bun.

One portion equals:
2 meats + 1 fat + 2 breads + 1/2 milk.

321 kilocalories   20 g proteins   38 g carbohydrates   12 g fat
36 mg cholesterol   6 g fiber   10 mg iron   204 mg calcium
141 mg magnesium   431 mg potassium   359 mg sodium

74

Vegetarian Stew

Preparation time: 10 minutes   Cooking time: 20 minutes
6 servings

Tofu, firm, in cubes	454 g	(1 pound)
Onion, minced	1	
Garlic, minced	1 clove	
Almonds, thin slices	60 ml	(1/4 cup)
Celery, cut on a diagonal	1 stalk	
Carrot, in thin round slices	1	
Potatoes, in small cubes	2	
Yellow or green beans	500 ml	(2 cups)
Broth of your choice	250 ml	(1 cup)
Flour, whole wheat	15 ml	(1 tbsp.)
Pepper, salt or no-salt shaker (pg. 155)	to taste	
Red kidney beans, cooked or chickpeas	540 ml	(1 x 19 oz can)

1. Put all ingredients (except the kidney beans or chickpeas) in a pot.
2. Mix well, cover, and cook for approx. 15 minutes.
3. Add the legumes and continue cooking for 5 minutes.
4. Serve over rice.

One portion equals:
2 meats + 2 vegetables + 1 bread + 1/2 milk.

299 kilocalories   22 g proteins   35 g carbohydrates   10 g fat
0 mg cholesterol   4 g fiber   11 mg iron   222 mg calcium
145 mg magnesium   920 mg potassium   166 mg sodium

Vegetables with Melted Cheese

Preparation time: 20 minutes   Cooking time: 20 minutes
4 servings

Vegetables, varied, fresh or frozen	1 L	(4 cups)
Milk (2% m.f. or less)	250 ml	(1 cup)
Broth, powder or cubes	5 ml	(1 tsp.)
Flour, whole wheat	30 ml	(2 tbsps.)
Shallot, minced	1	
Garlic powder	a pinch	
Basil, fresh, parsley, and onion powder	a pinch of each	
Pepper, salt or no-salt shaker (pg. 155)	to taste	
Cheese (20% m.f. or less), grated	125 ml	(1/2 cup)

1. Steam the fresh or frozen vegetables for approx. 10 minutes.
2. Put in a greased square baking pan for the oven.
3. Mix the 7 other ingredients (except the cheese) without making lumps.
4. Cook until thickened.
5. Pour this mixture over the vegetables.
6. Sprinkle with grated cheese.
7. Broil in the oven for approx. 5 to 10 minutes.

One portion equals:
1 vegetable + 1/2 meat + 1 milk.

141 kilocalories   12 g proteins   7 g carbohydrates   7 g fat
23 mg cholesterol   0 g fiber   0 mg iron   331 mg calcium
23 mg magnesium   148 mg potassium   218 mg sodium

Healthy Fries

Preparation time: 5 minutes   Cooking time: 25 minutes
1 serving

Potato, with skin, cut julienne style . . . . 1 medium
Canola oil, olive oil, or other . . . . 5 ml   (1 tsp.)
Paprika . . . . a pinch
Onion powder and garlic powder . . . . a pinch of each
Parsley, fresh . . . . a pinch
Pepper, salt or no-salt shaker (pg. 155) . . . . . . to taste

1. Mix the 6 ingredients and place on a lightly greased cookie sheet.
2. Bake uncovered in the oven at 220ºC (425ºF) for approx. 20-25 minutes.
3. Turn occasionally.
4. Serve.

One portion equals:
1 fat + 1 bread.

131 kilocalories   4 g proteins   19 g carbohydrates   5 g fat
0 mg cholesterol   5 g fiber   5 mg iron   47 mg calcium
36 mg magnesium   644 mg potassium   16 mg sodium

Thick Ham Stew

Preparation time: 15 minutes   Cooking time: 20 minutes
6 servings

Ham, cooked, in small pieces	500 ml	(2 cups)
Onion, minced	1	
Garlic, minced	1 clove	
Eggplant, cut into small pieces	1 medium	
Tomatoes, crushed	540 ml	(1 x 19 oz can)
Zucchini, in round slices	1 small	
Green pepper, in pieces	1	
Thyme, fresh, basil, oregano	a pinch of each	
Pepper, salt or no-salt shaker (pg. 155)	to taste	
Tomato juice	125 ml	(1/2 cup)

1. Cook all ingredients in a saucepan over low heat, uncovered without added fat for approx. 20 minutes.
2. Garnish with parsley.
3. Serve over rice, pasta, or on couscous.
4. Sprinkle with olive oil if desired (1 tsp. = 1 fat).

One portion equals:
3 meats + 2 vegetables.

195 kilocalories   22 g proteins   10 g carbohydrates   7 g fat
52 mg cholesterol   2 g fiber   2 mg iron   26 mg calcium
40 mg magnesium   722 mg potassium   1355 mg sodium

Chinese Liver

Preparation time: 10 minutes   Cooking time: 30 minutes
4 servings

Veal liver, raw, sliced	454 g	(1 pound)
Garlic, minced	1 clove	
Onion, in round slices	1	
Celery, cut on a diagonal	1 stalk	
Carrot, in thin round slices	1	
Chicken broth, defatted	125 ml	(1/2 cup)
Green pepper, in pieces	1	
Red pepper, in pieces	1	
Broccoli, raw, in florets	500 ml	(2 cups)
Soy sauce	30 ml	(2 tbsps.)
Parsley, fresh	for garnish	

1. Cook the first 5 ingredients in a pot over medium heat without added fat for approx. 10 minutes.
2. Moisten with some broth or water as needed.
3. Mix the 6 other ingredients and add to the liver.
4. Cover and continue cooking for approx. 10 minutes.
5. Serve with rice vermicelli or plain rice.

One portion equals:
3 meats + 2 vegetables.

221 kilocalories   24 g proteins   20 g carbohydrates   5 g fat
35 mg cholesterol   4 g fiber   7 mg iron   62 mg calcium
50 mg magnesium   824 mg potassium   624 mg sodium

79

Oriental Pork

Preparation time: 5 minutes   Cooking time: 20 minutes
4 servings

Pork, uncooked, in strips	454 g	(1 pound)
Onion, in round slices	1	
Celery, cut on a diagonal	1 stalk	
Carrots, in thin sticks	2 medium	
Soy sauce	45 ml	(3 tbsps.)
Broth of your choice	250 ml	(1 cup)
Flour, whole wheat	15 ml	(1 tbsp.)
Snow peas, cooked	500 ml	(2 cups)
Red pepper	1	
Ginger, fresh, chopped	15 ml	(1 tbsp.)
Pepper	to taste	

1. Cook the first 4 ingredients in a pot over medium heat without added fat for approx. 10 minutes.
2. Moisten with some broth or water as needed.
3. Mix the 7 other ingredients and add to the pork.
4. Cover and continue cooking over medium heat for approx. 10 minutes.
5. Serve over rice.

One portion equals:
3 meats + 2 vegetables.

221 kilocalories   31 g proteins   16 g carbohydrates   3 g fat
64 mg cholesterol   4 g fiber   4 mg iron   64 mg calcium
67 mg magnesium   850 mg potassium   903 mg sodium

Curried Pork Cutlets

Preparation time: 10 minutes   Cooking time: 25 minutes
4 servings

Pork cutlets, boneless, no fat	454 g	(1 pound)
Onion, chopped	1	
Garlic, minced	1 clove	
Celery, cut on a diagonal	2 stalks	
Carrots, in round slices	2	
Broth of your choice	250 ml	(1 cup)
Mushrooms, sliced	250 ml	(1 cup)
Red apple, in pieces	1	
Worcestershire sauce	15 ml	(1 tbsp.)
Brown sugar, sugar, honey, fructose or fruit purée .	5 ml	(1 tsp.)
Mustard, dried	5 ml	(1 tsp.)
Curry powder	2 ml	(1/2 tsp.)

1. Cook the first 5 ingredients in a pot over medium heat without added fat for approx. 10 minutes.
2. Moisten with some broth or water as needed.
3. Mix the 7 other ingredients and add to the chops.
4. Cover and continue cooking over medium heat for approx. 10 minutes.
5. Serve over rice.

One portion equals:
3 meats + 2 vegetables + 1/4 fruit.

211 kilocalories   23 g proteins   17 g carbohydrates   6 g fat
51 mg cholesterol   3 g fiber 2 mg iron   62 mg calcium
44 mg magnesium   818 mg potassium   328 mg sodium

Chinese Ham

Preparation time: 30 minutes   Cooking time: 15 minutes
6 servings

Carrots, in thin round slices	2	
Green pepper, in strips	1	
Garlic, minced	1 clove	
Shallots, thin slices	2	
Mushrooms, sliced	500 ml	(2 cups)
Snow peas, cooked or broccoli florets	250 ml	(1 cup)
Chicken broth, defatted or other	125 ml	(1/2 cup)
Ham, cut julienne style	500 ml	(2 cups)
Soy sauce	15 ml	(1 tbsp.)
Ginger, fresh, chopped	15 ml	(1 tbsp.)
Pepper	to taste	

1. Cook the vegetables with broth in a pan over medium heat until tender, approx. 10 minutes.
2. Add the ham, soy sauce, and seasonings.
3. Continue cooking uncovered over low heat for approx. 5 minutes.
4. Serve with rice.

One portion equals:
3 meats + 1 vegetable.

194 kilocalories   22 g proteins   9 g carbohydrates   7 g fat
52 mg cholesterol   2 g fiber   3 mg iron   33 mg calcium
36 mg magnesium   655 mg potassium   1489 mg sodium

Baked Pork Cutlets

Preparation time: 15 minutes   Cooking time: 35 minutes
4 servings

Pork cutlets, boneless, no fat	454 g	(1 pound)
Onion, minced	1	
Worcestershire sauce	5 ml	(1 tsp.)
Tomato juice	125 ml	(1/2 cup)
Basil	5 ml	(1 tsp.)
Parsley	a pinch	
Cayenne pepper	a pinch	
Thyme	a pinch	
Oregano	a pinch	
Sugar, brown or white	5 ml	(1 tsp.)
Broth of your choice	125 ml	(1/2 cup)

1. Cook the cutlets and onion in a frying pan over medium heat without added fat for approx. 5 minutes.
2. Add tomato juice as needed.
3. Put in a greased rectangular pan for the oven.
4. Mix the remaining ingredients and pour onto the chops.
5. Bake uncovered in the oven at 180ºC (350ºF) for approx. 30 minutes.
6. Serve with a salad or your choice of vegetables.

One portion equals:
3 meats + 1 vegetable.

162 kilocalories   22 g proteins   7 g carbohydrates   5 g fat
51 mg cholesterol   1 g fiber   1 mg iron   41 mg calcium
32 mg magnesium   568 mg potassium   278 mg sodium

Crunchy Pizza

Preparation time: 10 minutes   Cooking time: 20 minutes
4 servings

Bread, whole wheat or your choice of bread . . . 8 slices

Tomato sauce or pizza sauce	80 ml	(1/3 cup)
Ham, pieces	125 ml	(1/2 cup)
Green pepper, in pieces	1	
Shallots, thin slices	2	
Cheese (20% m.f. or less), grated	180 ml	(3/4 cup)

1. On each slice of bread, add the other ingredients in order.
2. Bake in the oven uncovered at 180ºC (350ºF) for approx. 20 minutes.
3. Serve.

One portion equals:
2 meats + 2 breads + 1/2 milk.

352 kilocalories   27 g proteins   32 g carbohydrates   14 g fat
46 mg cholesterol   5 g fiber   3 mg iron   412 mg calcium
76 mg magnesium   464 mg potassium   1161 mg sodium

Quiche Lorraine

Preparation time: 10 minutes   Cooking time: 55 minutes
6 servings

HEALTHY PIE CRUST

Flour, whole wheat	500 ml	(2 cups)
Oil, non hydrogenated margarine, or butter	60 ml	(1/4 cup)
Yogurt, plain (2% m.f. or less)	180 ml	(3/4 cup)
Water	30 ml	(2 tbsps.)
Milk (2% m.f. or less)	250 ml	(1 cup)
Cheese (20% m.f. or less), grated	250 ml	(1 cup)
Ham or chicken, cooked, in pieces	250 ml	(1 cup)
Eggs, medium	4	
Onion, minced	1	
Worcestershire sauce	2 ml	(1/2 tsp.)
Nutmeg	a pinch	
Pepper, salt or no-salt shaker (pg. 155)	to taste	

1. Prepare the pastry following the instructions (pg. 142).
2. Mix the remaining ingredients and pour into the uncooked undercrust.
3. Bake uncovered in the oven at 180ºC (350ºF) for approx. 45 to 55 minutes.
4. Serve.

One portion equals:
3 meats + 2 fat + 2 breads + 1 milk.

533 kilocalories   36 g proteins   40 g carbohydrates   26 g fat
20 mg cholesterol   6 g fiber   3 mg iron   477 mg calcium
96 mg magnesium   606 mg potassium   965 mg sodium

Sandwich Topping

Preparation time: 5 minutes   Cooking time: none
1 serving

Chicken or turkey, cooked, ground	60 ml	(1/4 cup)
Red pepper, chopped	15 ml	(1 tbsp.)
Garlic powder, tarragon, salt and pepper ...	a pinch of each	
Mayonnaise, light (pg. 33)	15 ml	(1 tbsp.)
Bread, whole wheat	2 slices	

1. Mix all ingredients.
2. Fill your choice of bread with this mixture.
3. Serve.

One portion equals:
2 meats + 2 breads.

270 kilocalories   20 g proteins   28 g carbohydrates   9 g fat
39 mg cholesterol   4 g fiber   2 mg iron   48 mg calcium
61 mg magnesium   252 mg potassium   432 mg sodium

Meatball Stew

Preparation time: 30 minutes   Cooking time: 2 1/2 hours
4 servings

Pig's feet	2	
Water	2 L	(8 cups)
Beef, veal or pork, lean ground	454 g	(1 pound)
Garlic powder	a pinch	
Cinnamon, cloves, and nutmeg	a pinch of each	
Onion, minced	1	
Broth from the feet, defatted	500 ml	(2 cups)
Cinnamon	a pinch	
Cloves, ground	a pinch	
Nutmeg	a pinch	
Pepper, salt or no-salt shaker (pg. 155)	to taste	
Broth from the feet, defatted	60 ml	(1/4 cup)
Flour, whole wheat, grilled	30 ml	(2 tbsps.)

1. Cook the pig's feet uncovered in water over medium heat for approx. 2 hours.
2. During this time, mix the meat and the seasonings.
3. Form this meat mixture into 20 meatballs (5 per portion).
4. De-bone the feet once they are cooked and refrigerate the broth. Then defat.
5. In a saucepan, put the 6 other ingredients and the pig's feet meat.
6. Bring to a boil and put the meatballs in the broth.
7. Cover and cook over medium heat for approx. 30 minutes.
8. Mix the flour and the broth without making lumps.
9. Add at the end of cooking to thicken. Serve or freeze.

One portion equals:
3 1/2 meats + 1/2 bread.

209 kilocalories   30 g proteins   7 g carbohydrates   6 g fat
51 mg cholesterol   1 g fiber   2 mg iron   27 mg calcium
40 mg magnesium   683 mg potassium   533 mg sodium

Baked Ham

Preparation time: 15 minutes   Cooking time: 2 1/2 hours
4 servings

Ham, whole, boned	454 g	(1 pound)
Onion, minced	1	
Water	4 L	(16 cups)
Cloves, ground	1 ml	(1/4 tsp.)
Maple sugar or brown sugar	60 ml	(1/4 cup)
Onion powder and garlic powder	a pinch of each	
Mustard, dried	10 ml	(2 tsps.)
Pepper, salt or no-salt shaker (pg. 155)	to taste	
Broth of ham, defatted	15 ml	(1 tbsp.)
Broth of ham, defatted	250 ml	(1 cup)
Flour, whole wheat	15 ml	(1 tbsp.)

1. Put the ham, onion, and water in a saucepan.
2. Cover and cook over a slow heat for approx. 2 hours.
3. Once cooked, remove the ham and drain the fat.
4. Put the ham in a roaster with a grill at the bottom.
5. Mix the next 6 ingredients and uniformly brush onto the ham.
6. Bake uncovered in the oven at 170ºC (325ºF) for approx. 20 minutes.
7. Remove the ham from the roaster.
8. Mix the broth and flour without making lumps.
9. Pour this mixture into the bottom of the roaster and bring to a boil to thicken the sauce.
10. Put the sauce in a small pot or a gravy-boat.
11. Serve with some sauce, a salad, or your choice of vegetables.

One portion equals:
3 meats.

224 kilocalories   27 g proteins   7 g carbohydrates   9 g fat
65 mg cholesterol   1 g fiber   2 mg iron   32 mg calcium
35 mg magnesium   539 mg potassium   1793 mg sodium

Fish Steak

Preparation time: 10 minutes   Cooking time: 10 minutes
4 servings

Fish steaks of your choice (1 steak = 120 g) . . . . . 454 g   (1 pound)
Butter, non hydrogenated margarine, or oil   . . . . . . 5 ml   (1 tsp.)

Beef broth or broth of your choice or orange juice . . 45 ml   (3 tbsps.)
Tarragon or basil . . . . a pinch
Garlic, minced . . . . 1 clove
Pepper, salt or no-salt shaker (pg. 155) . . . . to taste

Parsley, fresh   . . . . for garnish

1. Cook the steaks (slices of fish) with oil in a frying pan for approx. 5 minutes.
2. Mix the other ingredients and add to the steaks.
3. Continue cooking for approx. 5 minutes.
4. Trim with parsley and serve with your choice of salad or vegetables.

One portion equals:
4 meats.

143 kilocalories   28 g proteins   0 g carbohydrate   3 g fat
80 mg cholesterol   0 g fiber   0 mg iron   23 mg calcium
66 mg magnesium   400 mg potassium   166 mg sodium

Breaded Fish Fillets

Preparation time: 5 minutes   Cooking time: 15 minutes
4 servings

Fish fillets of your choice	454 g	(1 pound)
Lemon juice	15 ml	(1 tbsp.)
Breadcrumbs	80 ml	(1/3 cup)
Savory, ground	a pinch	
Pepper, salt or no-salt shaker (pg. 155)	a pinch	
Paprika	to your taste	

1. Spread the lemon juice onto the fillets.
2. Mix the breadcrumbs and seasonings.
3. Cover the fish fillets with the seasoned breadcrumbs.
4. Sprinkle with paprika.
5. Put the fillets in a greased rectangular pan for the oven.
6. Bake in the oven uncovered at 180ºC (350ºF) for approx. 15 minutes.
7. Serve with lemon juice or a cheese sauce (pg. 34).
8. Accompany with rice and a salad.

One portion equals:
3 meats + 1/2 bread.

144 kilocalories   23 g proteins   8 g carbohydrates   2 g fat
54 mg cholesterol   0 g fiber   1 mg iron   44 mg calcium
40 mg magnesium   437 mg potassium   179 mg sodium

Salmon and Broccoli Squares

Preparation time: 10 minutes   Cooking time: 35 minutes
6 servings

Eggs, beaten	2	
Salmon, in water, drained	368 g	(2 x 6 1/2 oz can)
Broccoli, raw, in florets	250 ml	(1 cup)
Cottage cheese (1% m.f.)	250 ml	(1 cup)
Onion, minced	1	
Green pepper, chopped	15 ml	(1 tbsp.)
Breadcrumbs	30 ml	(2 tbsps.)
Pepper, salt or no-salt shaker (pg. 155)	to taste	
Cheese (20% m.f. or less), grated	250 ml	(1 cup)

1. Mix all the ingredients except the grated cheese.
2. Put in a greased square baking pan for the oven.
3. Spread evenly with grated cheese.
4. Bake in the oven uncovered at 180°C (350°F) for approx. 35 minutes.
5. Serve with a white sauce (pg. 34).
6. Accompany with a salad or vegetables of your choice.

One portion equals:
3 meats + 1 milk.

301 kilocalories   37 g proteins   8 g carbohydrates   13 g fat
39 mg cholesterol   1 g fiber   1 mg iron   398 mg calcium
44 mg magnesium   460 mg potassium   509 mg sodium

Fillets of Sole with Almonds

Preparation time: 5 minutes   Cooking time: 15 minutes
4 servings

Sole fillets . . . . 454 g   (1 pound)
Flour, whole wheat or other . . . . 60 ml   (1/4 cup)
Pepper, salt or no-salt shaker (pg. 155) . . . . . . to taste

Butter, non hydrogenated margarine, or oil . . . . 5 ml   (1 tsp.)

Almonds, grilled, thin slices . . . . 60 ml   (1/4 cup)

1. Cover the sole fillets with flour.
2. Cook the fillets uncovered over medium heat in a lightly greased frying pan for approx. 10 minutes.
3. Add the almonds and continue cooking for 2 minutes.
4. Serve plain or with a white sauce (pg. 34).

One portion equals:
3 meats + 1 fat.

192 kilocalories   24 g proteins   8 g carbohydrates   7 g fat
57 mg cholesterol   1 g fiber   1 mg iron   49 mg calcium
74 mg magnesium   512 mg potassium   103 mg sodium

92

Tuna Noodle Casserole

Preparation time: 5 minutes   Cooking time: 10 minutes
4 servings

Milk (2% m.f. or less)	500 ml	(2 cups)
Flour, whole wheat or other	60 ml	(1/4 cup)
Onion, minced	1	
Tuna, canned in water, drained	368 g	(2 x 6 1/2 oz can)
Pepper, salt or no-salt shaker (pg. 155)	to taste	
Tarragon	a pinch	
Egg noodles, cooked, of your choice	500 ml	(2 cups)

1. Mix the milk, flour, and onion without making lumps.
2. Put in a saucepan.
3. Cook over medium heat for approx. 5 minutes until thickened.
4. Add the other ingredients and continue cooking for approx. 5 minutes.
5. Serve with a salad or your choice of vegetables.

One portion equals:
3 meats + 1 bread + 1/2 milk.

337 kilocalories   32 g proteins   37 g carbohydrates   7 g fat
76 mg cholesterol   4 g fiber   3 mg iron   191 mg calcium
79 mg magnesium   543 mg potassium   419 mg sodium

Wrapped Fish Fillets

Preparation time: 5 minutes   Cooking time: 20 minutes
4 servings

Fish fillets of your choice	454 g	(1 pound)
Lemon juice	15 ml	(1 tbsp.)
Garlic, minced	1 clove	
Shallot, minced	1	
Basil, fresh	a pinch	
Pepper, salt or no-salt shaker (pg. 155)	to taste	
Celery, chopped	1 stalk	
Red pepper, in small pieces	1/2	
Tomato	4 slices	
Lemon	4 slices	

1. Put the fillets in aluminum foil.
2. Add the 9 other ingredients onto the fish.
3. Hermetically seal the aluminum foil.
4. Bake in the oven at 160ºC (325ºF) for approx. 20 minutes.
5. Serve with a salad.

One portion equals:
3 meats.

113 kilocalories   22 g proteins   2 g carbohydrates   1 g fat
54 mg cholesterol   0 g fiber   1 mg iron   28 mg calcium
39 mg magnesium   483 mg potassium   101 mg sodium

Fish Fillets with Melted Cheese

Preparation time: 5 minutes   Cooking time: 20 minutes
4 servings

Fish fillets of your choice	454 g	(1 pound)
Butter, non hydrogenated margarine, or oil	5 ml	(1 tsp.)
Paprika	5 ml	(1 tsp.)
Broth of your choice	60 ml	(1/4 cup)
Milk (2% m.f. or less)	60 ml	(1/4 cup)
Flour, whole wheat	30 ml	(2 tbsps.)
Pepper, salt or no-salt shaker (pg. 155)	to taste	
Parsley, fresh	30 ml	(2 tbsps.)
Cheese (20% m.f. or less), grated	125 ml	(1/2 cup)

1. Put the fillets in a greased rectangular pan for the oven.
2. Mix the other ingredients, except the cheese.
3. Cook the mixture in a small saucepan over medium heat until thickened.
4. Pour over the fillets.
5. Cover with grated cheese.
6. Bake uncovered in the oven at 180ºC (350ºF) for approx. 10 minutes.
7. Broil in the oven for approx. 5 minutes.
8. Serve with vegetables or a salad.

One portion equals:
3 meats + 1/2 milk.

232 kilocalories   32 g proteins   5 g carbohydrates   9 g fat
77 mg cholesterol   1 g fiber   1 mg iron   296 mg calcium
54 mg magnesium   514 mg potassium   342 mg sodium

Salmon Loaf

Preparation time: 20 minutes   Cooking time: 35 minutes
4 servings

Salmon, flaked, drained	368 g	(2 x 6 1/2 oz)
Oatmeal, raw	125 ml	(1/2 cup)
Milk (2% m.f. or less)	30 ml	(2 tbsps.)
Eggs, beaten	2	
Shallot, minced	1 ml	(1/4 tsp.)
Green or red pepper	1	
Oregano, fresh, thyme, basil	a pinch of each	
Pepper, salt or no-salt shaker (pg. 155)	to taste	

1. Mix all ingredients and put in a greased bread pan.
2. Bake uncovered in the oven at 180ºC (350ºF) for approx. 35 minutes.
3. Serve with a white sauce (pg. 34).
4. Serve with an attractive salad.

One portion equals:
3 meats + 1/2 bread.

240 kilocalories   29 g proteins   12 g carbohydrates   8 g fat
17 mg cholesterol   2 g fiber   2 mg iron   48 mg calcium
58 mg magnesium   546 mg potassium   116 mg sodium

Coquilles Saint-Jacques

Preparation time: 20 minutes   Cooking time: 20 minutes
4 servings

Scallops	16 small	
Shrimp	16 small	
Milk (2% m.f. or less)	for cooking	
Flour, whole wheat or other	60 ml	(1/4 cup)
Milk (2% m.f. or less)	250 ml	(1 cup)
Red wine or apple juice	60 ml	(1/4 cup)
Mushrooms, in pieces	250 ml	(1 cup)
Shallot, minced	1	
Garlic powder, oregano, parsley	a pinch of each	
Pepper, salt or no-salt shaker (pg. 155)	to taste	
Potatoes, mashed	for decoration	
Cheese (20% m.f. or less), grated	180 ml	(3/4 cup)

1. Put the scallops and shrimp in a saucepan covered with milk and cook over medium heat (5 minutes).
2. Strain the seafood and set it aside.
3. Mix the 7 other ingredients in a bowl without making lumps. Put in a saucepan.
4. Cook over medium heat until thickened.
5. Add the scallops and shrimp.
6. Continue cooking for approx. 5 minutes. Put in the greased shells.
7. Decorate the rim of each shell with mashed potato.
8. Sprinkle with grated cheese.
9. Broil in the oven for approx. 5 minutes. Serve.

One portion equals:
2 meats + 1 milk.

233 kilocalories   21 g proteins   12 g carbohydrates   10 g fat
39 mg cholesterol   1 g fiber   1 mg iron   450 mg calcium
50 mg magnesium   340 mg potassium   334 mg sodium

Omelet

Preparation time: 5 minutes   Cooking time: 10 minutes
6 servings

Eggs	8	
Milk (2% m.f. or less)	250 ml	(1 cup)
Shallot, minced	1	
Thyme, fresh, oregano, basil	a pinch of each	
Pepper, salt or no-salt shaker (pg. 155)	to taste	
Vegetables, varied of your choice, cooked	250 ml	(1 cup)
Cheese (20% m.f. or less), grated	250 ml	(1 cup)

1. Mix all ingredients with a mixer. Put in a lightly greased frying pan.
2. Cook over medium heat for approx. 10 minutes.
3. Turn and continue cooking until medium-well done.
4. Serve.

One portion equals:
2 meats + 1 milk.

262 kilocalories   23 g proteins   7 g carbohydrates   15 g fat
31 mg cholesterol   0 g fiber   1 mg iron   427 mg calcium
29 mg magnesium   274 mg potassium   390 mg sodium

Crêpe

Preparation time: 5 minutes   Cooking time: 5 minutes
4 servings

Milk (2% m.f. or less)	250 ml	(1 cup)
Egg, beaten	1	
Baking powder	5 ml	(1 tsp.)
Flour, whole wheat	250 ml	(1 cup)
Vanilla	1 ml	(1/4 tsp.)
Butter, non hydrogenated margarine, or oil	5 ml	(1 tsp.)

1. Mix all ingredients (except the fat) with a mixer in a bowl.
2. Cook 60 ml (1/4 cup) of batter per pancake over medium to high heat in a lightly greased frying pan.
3. Serve.

One portion equals:
1/2 fat + 1 bread + 1/2 milk.

169 kilocalories 8 g proteins 27 g carbohydrates 4 g fat
61 mg cholesterol 4 g fiber 1 mg iron 125 mg calcium
54 mg magnesium 246 mg potassium 125 mg sodium

Shrimp Fettuccini

Preparation time: 10 minutes   Cooking time: 20 minutes
4 servings

Fettuccini, whole wheat, uncooked	227 g	(1/2 pound)
Onion, chopped	1	
Garlic, chopped	1 clove	
Mushrooms, sliced	250 ml	(1 cup)
Broccoli, raw, in florets	500 ml	(2 cups)
Red pepper, in strips	2	
Tomato, in pieces	1	
Chicken broth, defatted	125 ml	(1/2 cup)
Shrimp, cooked	454 g	(1 pound)
Parmesan cheese (20% m.f. or less), grated . .	60 ml	(1/4 cup)
Milk (2% m.f. or less)	500 ml	(2 cups)
Flour of your choice	45 ml	(3 tbsps.)
Orange zest	30 ml	(2 tbsps.)
Curry and parsley	to taste	
Pepper, salt or no-salt shaker (pg. 155)	to taste	

1. Cook the fettuccini in water (1.5 Liters-6 cups) for approx. 8 to 10 minutes.
2. Strain and rinse with cold water.
3. In a saucepan, cook the 6 vegetables with the broth for 5 minutes over medium heat.
4. Mix the other ingredients in a bowl.
5. Add this mixture to the vegetables, cook until thickened.
6. Continue cooking over medium heat for approx. 5 minutes.
7. Serve over fettuccini.
8. Serve with an attractive salad.

One portion equals:
3 meats + 2 vegetables + 2 breads + 1/2 milk.

345 kilocalories   36 g proteins   42 g carbohydrates   5 g fat
23 mg cholesterol   4 g fiber   6 mg iron   261 mg calcium
107 mg magnesium   970 mg potassium   443 mg sodium

Fettuccini Alfredo

Preparation time: 10 minutes   Cooking time: 15 minutes
4 servings

Fettuccini, whole wheat, uncooked	227 g	(1/2 pound)
Parmesan cheese (20% m.f. or less), grated . .	125 ml	(1/2 cup)
Milk (2% m.f. or less)	500 ml	(2 cups)
Sour cream (14% m.f.)	125 ml	(1/2 cup)
Flour of your choice	30 ml	(2 tbsps.)
Onion powder and garlic powder	a pinch of each	
Pepper, salt or no-salt shaker (pg. 155)	to taste	

1. Cook the fettuccini in water (1.5 Liters-6 cups) for approx. 10 minutes.
2. Strain and rinse in cold water.
3. Mix the remaining ingredients without making lumps.
4. Put in a saucepan and cook until thickened, approx. 10 minutes.
5. Remove from heat.
6. Serve over fettuccini.
7. Serve with an attractive salad.

One portion equals:
1/2 meat + 1 fat + 1 bread + 1/2 milk.

195 kilocalories   9 g proteins   26 g carbohydrates   7 g fat
22 mg cholesterol   0 g fiber   1 mg iron   198 mg calcium
39 mg magnesium   268 mg potassium   79 mg sodium

Lasagna

Preparation time: 20 minutes   Cooking time: 150 minutes
8 servings

Beef or veal, lean ground	454 g	(1 pound)
Onion, minced	1	
Celery, in pieces	1 stalk	
Garlic, minced	1 clove	
Mushrooms, sliced	250 ml	(1 cup)
Tomato paste	156 ml	(1 x 5 1/2 oz can)
Cream of tomato soup	284 ml	(1 x 10 oz can)
Vegetable juice	1.36 L	(1 x 48 oz can)
Basil, fresh	30 ml	(2 tbsps.)
Bay leaf	3	
Pepper, salt or no-salt shaker (pg. 155)	to taste	
Lasagna noodles, cooked	9	
Cheese (20% m.f. or less), grated	375 ml	(1 1/2 cups)

1. Cook the first 4 ingredients in a pot over medium heat without added fat for approx. 10 minutes.
2. Moisten with some broth or water as needed.
3. Mix the 7 other ingredients and put in the pot.
4. Cook uncovered over slow heat for approx. 2 hours.
5. Put some sauce in a greased rectangular pan for the oven.
6. Layer the lasagna noodles and sauce.
7. Cover with grated cheese.
8. Bake in the oven at 180ºC (350ºF) for approx. 35-40 minutes.
9. Serve with an attractive salad.

One portion equals:
3 meats + 1 vegetable + 1 bread + 1 milk.

360 kilocalories   32 g proteins   32 g carbohydrates   12 g fat
49 mg cholesterol   4 g fiber   3 mg iron   409 mg calcium
65 mg magnesium   659 mg potassium   452 mg sodium

Chinese Macaroni

Preparation time: 15 minutes   Cooking time: 30 minutes
4 servings

Macaroni, whole wheat, uncooked	250 ml	(1 cup)
Beef or veal, lean ground	454 g	(1 pound)
Onion, minced	1	
Celery, in pieces	1 stalk	
Carrot, cubed	1	
Soy sauce	30 ml	(2 tbsps.)
Garlic powder	2 ml	(1/2 tsp.)
Pepper, fine herbs	to taste	
Green pepper, in strips	1	
Red pepper, in strips	1	
Mushrooms, sliced	500 ml	(2 cups)

1. Cook the macaroni in boiling water (1.5 Liters-6 cups) for approx. 10 minutes.
2. Strain and rinse with cold water.
3. Cook the next 4 ingredients in a pot over medium heat without added fat.
4. Moisten with some broth or water as needed.
5. Mix the 6 other ingredients and put in the pot, continue cooking for approx. 20 minutes.
6. Add the macaroni and mix well.
7. Serve.

One portion equals:
3 meats + 2 vegetables + 1 1/2 breads.

310 kilocalories   31 g proteins   35 g carbohydrates   6 g fat
43 mg cholesterol   3 g fiber   4 mg iron   45 mg calcium
84 mg magnesium   1012 mg potassium   497 mg sodium

Italian Spaghetti Sauce

Preparation time: 15 minutes   Cooking time: 3 hours
6 servings

Beef or veal, lean ground	454 g	(1 pound)
Onion, minced	1	
Garlic, minced	1 clove	
Red pepper, chopped	1	
Celery, cut on a diagonal	1 stalk	
Carrot, in pieces	1	
Mushrooms	250 ml	(1 cup)
Worcestershire sauce	5 ml	(1 tsp.)
Soy sauce	15 ml	(1 tbsp.)
Tomato paste	156 ml	(1 x 5 1/2 oz can)
Tomatoes, diced	540 ml	(1 x 19 oz can)
Vegetable juice	1.36 L	(1 x 48 oz can)
Basil, fresh	15 ml	(1 tbsp.)
Thyme, fresh, oregano, and cayenne pepper	a pinch of each	
Bay leaf	3	
Pepper, salt or no-salt shaker (pg. 155)	to taste	

1. Cook the first 3 ingredients in a pot over medium heat without added fat for approx. 10 minutes.
2. Moisten with some broth or water as needed.
3. Drain off the excess fat.
4. Mix the 13 other ingredients and put in the pot.
5. Cook uncovered over slow heat for approx. 2 1/2 to 3 hours.
6. Stir occasionally.
7. Serve with spaghetti, bean sprouts, or spaghetti squash.

One portion equals:
2 meats + 2 vegetables + 1 fat.

174 kilocalories   19 g proteins   16 g carbohydrates   4 g fat
29 mg cholesterol   4 g fiber   3 mg iron   35 mg calcium
51 mg magnesium   998 mg potassium   168 mg sodium

Macaroni and Cheese

Preparation time: 10 minutes   Cooking time: 15 minutes
4 servings

Macaroni, whole wheat, uncooked	250 ml	(1 cup)
Shallot, minced	1	
Milk (2% m.f. or less)	500 ml	(2 cups)
Flour of your choice	30 ml	(2 tbsps.)
Parmesan cheese (20% m.f. or less), grated . .	125 ml	(1/2 cup)
Mozzarella cheese (20% m.f. or less), grated . .	125 ml	(1/2 cup)
Parsley, fresh	30 ml	(2 tbsps.)
Onion powder	a pinch	
Pepper, salt or no-salt shaker (pg. 155)	to taste	

1. Cook the macaroni in boiling water (1.5 Liters-6 cups) for approx.
   10 minutes.
2. Strain and rinse with cold water.
3. Mix the 8 other ingredients in a bowl.
4. Add to a saucepan and cook until thickened.
5. Let simmer for approx. 2 minutes.
6. Add the macaroni and continue cooking for 2 minutes.
7. Serve.

One portion equals:
1 meat + 1 bread + 1 milk.

272 kilocalories   18 g proteins   31 g carbohydrates   9 g fat
28 mg cholesterol   0 g fiber   1 mg iron   422 mg calcium
68 mg magnesium   306 mg potassium   249 mg sodium

Italian Macaroni

Preparation time: 15 minutes   Cooking time: 40 minutes
4 servings

Macaroni, whole wheat, uncooked	250 ml	(1 cup)
Beef or veal, lean ground	454 g	(1 pound)
Onion, minced	1	
Garlic, minced	1 clove	
Celery, in pieces	1 stalk	
Tomatoes, in pieces	540 ml	(1 x 19 oz can)
Parsley, fresh, chopped	15 ml	(1 tbsp.)
Oregano, fresh	2 ml	(1/2 tsp.)
Basil, fresh	5 ml	(1 tsp.)
Thyme, fresh	a pinch	
Pepper, salt or no-salt shaker (pg. 155)	to taste	

1. Cook the macaroni in boiling water (1.5 Liters - 6 cups) for approx. 10 minutes.
2. Rinse and strain.
3. Cook the next 4 ingredients in a pot over medium heat without added fat for approx. 10 minutes.
4. Moisten with some broth or water as needed.
5. Mix the 6 other ingredients and put in the pot, continue cooking for approx. 20 minutes.
6. Add the macaroni and mix well.
7. Serve.

One portion equals:
3 meats + 2 vegetables + 1 bread.

294 kilocalories   30 g proteins   31 g carbohydrates   6 g fat
43 mg cholesterol   2 g fiber   3 mg iron   41 mg calcium
84 mg magnesium   942 mg potassium   81 mg sodium

106

Healthy Pizza of Your Choice

Preparation time: 30 minutes   Cooking time: 20 minutes
8 servings

Flour, whole wheat	250 ml	(1 cup)
Bread flour or rye flour	250 ml	(1 cup)
Yeast, active, dry, fast, and instant	15 ml	(1 tbsp.)
Salt	a pinch	
Milk (2% m.f. or less), hot but not boiling or water	125 ml	(1/2 cup)
Hot water	125 ml	(1/2 cup)
Butter, non hydrogenated margarine, or oil	15 ml	(1 tbsp.)
Pizza sauce or other flavor	125 ml	(1/2 cup)
Vegetables, varied, or another healthy topping	125 ml	(1/2 cup)
Cheese (20% m.f. or less)	250 ml	(1 cup)

1. Mix the first 4 ingredients in a large bowl.
2. Mix the milk, water, and fat. Add to the first mixture.
3. Knead this pastry mixture for approx. 5 minutes. Add flour as needed (dough no longer sticky).
4. Put the pastry in a well-greased patter and let swell for 15 minutes in a warm place.
5. Punch the pastry dough and knead for 4 minutes.
6. With a rolling pin or your hands, put on a cookie sheet.
7. Allow to swell slightly for approx. 10 minutes.
8. Add the sauce, your choice of topping, and the cheese onto the pizza crust.
9. Bake in the oven at 180ºC (350ºF) for approx. 20 minutes. Serve.

One portion equals:
1 meat + 1 vegetable + 1 bread + 1/2 milk.

245 kilocalories   15 g proteins   29 g carbohydrates   8 g fat
26 mg cholesterol   3 g fiber   2 mg iron   267 mg calcium
43 mg magnesium   259 mg potassium   304 mg sodium

Chicken and Rice

Preparation time: 15 minutes   Cooking time: 25 minutes
4 servings

Brown rice, long grain, cooked	250 ml	(1 cup)
Broth of your choice	375 ml	(1 1/2 cups)
Butter, non hydrogenated margarine, or oil	10 ml	(2 tsps.)
Chicken, uncooked, cut in pieces	250 ml	(1 cup)
Onion, minced	1	
Celery, in pieces	1 stalk	
Carrot, finely chopped	1	
Green pepper, chopped	1	
Chicken broth, defatted	60 ml	(1/4 cup)
Soy sauce	30 ml	(2 tbsps.)

Pepper, salt or no-salt shaker (pg. 155) . . . .   to taste

1. Cover and let simmer the first 3 ingredients over low heat for approx. 25 minutes.
2. Remove from the heat and set aside.
3. Cook the 8 other ingredients in a frying pan.
4. Add to the cooked rice and stir lightly.
5. Serve cold or hot.

One portion equals:
2 meats + 1 vegetable + 1 bread.

209 kilocalories 19 g proteins 21 g carbohydrates 5 g fat
46 mg cholesterol 3 g fiber 1 mg iron 42 mg calcium
49 mg magnesium 427 mg potassium 853 mg sodium

108

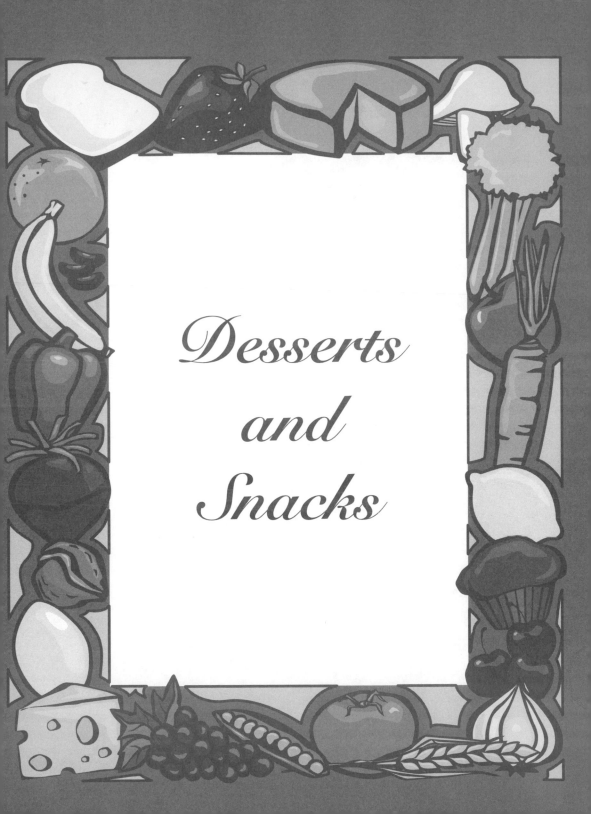

Desserts

and

Snacks

Healthy Muffins

Preparation time: 10 minutes   Cooking time: 20 minutes
12 servings

Egg	1	
Butter, non hydrogenated margarine, or oil	30 ml	(2 tbsps.)
Dates, dried, in small pieces	125 ml	(1/2 cup)
Apples, in small pieces	2	
Sunflower seeds or pumpkin seeds (ground)	60 ml	(1/4 cup)
Cinnamon	1 ml	(1/4 tsp.)
Salt	a pinch	
Milk (2% m.f. or less)	250 ml	(1 cup)
Flour, whole wheat with kamut flour, rye or oat flour	500 ml	(2 cups)
Baking powder	15 ml	(1 tbsp.)

1. Mix the first 8 ingredients with a mixer by adding them one by one in the order indicated.
2. In another bowl, mix the flour (2 choices if possible) and baking powder together.
3. Add this mixture to the first mixture and stir lightly until it is homogeneous.
4. Fill a lightly greased pan for 12 muffins.
5. Bake in the oven at 200°C (400°F) for approx. 20 minutes.
6. Serve.

One portion equals:
1 fat + 1 bread + 1 fruit.

160 kilocalories   5 g proteins   27 g carbohydrates   5 g fat
25 mg cholesterol   4 g fiber   1 mg iron   71 mg calcium
40 mg magnesium   218 mg potassium   103 mg sodium

Pineapple Muffins

Preparation time: 10 minutes   Cooking time: 20 minutes
12 servings

Egg	1	
Butter, non hydrogenated margarine, or oil	60 ml	(1/4 cup)
Brown sugar, sugar, honey, fructose or fruit purée	80 ml	(1/3 cup)
Pineapple pieces with juice	540 ml	(1 x 19 oz can)
Nutmeg	1 ml	(1/4 tsp.)
Salt	a pinch	
Milk (2% m.f. or less)	60 ml	(1/4 cup)
Flour, whole wheat with kamut flour, rye or oat flour	500 ml	(2 cups)
Baking powder	15 ml	(1 tbsp.)

1. Mix the first 7 ingredients with a mixer by adding them one by one in the order indicated.
2. In another bowl, mix the flour (2 choices if possible) and baking powder together.
3. Add this mixture to the first mixture and stir lightly until it is homogeneous.
4. Fill a lightly greased pan for 12 muffins.
5. Bake in the oven at 200ºC (400ºF) for approx. 15-20 minutes.
6. Serve.

One portion equals:
1 fat + 1 bread + 1 fruit.

166 kilocalories   4 g proteins   29 g carbohydrates   5 g fat
29 mg cholesterol   3 g fiber   1 mg iron   53 mg calcium
37 mg magnesium   160 mg potassium   115 mg sodium

Banana Muffins

Preparation time: 10 minutes   Cooking time: 20 minutes
12 servings

Egg	1	
Butter, non hydrogenated margarine, or oil	30 ml	(2 tbsps.)
Brown sugar, sugar, honey, fructose or fruit purée . .	80 ml	(1/3 cup)
Bananas, ripe, mashed	3	
Walnuts, chopped	80 ml	(1/3 cup)
Salt	a pinch	
Milk (2% m.f. or less)	60 ml	(1/4 cup)
Flour, whole wheat with kamut flour, rye or oat flour .	500 ml	(2 cups)
Baking powder	15 ml	(1 tbsp.)

1. Mix the first 7 ingredients with a mixer by adding them one by one in the order indicated.
2. In another bowl, mix the flour (2 choices if possible) and baking powder together.
3. Add this mixture to the first mixture and stir lightly until it is homogeneous.
4. Fill a lightly greased pan for 12 muffins.
5. Bake in the oven at 200ºC (400ºF) for approx. 15-20 minutes.
6. Serve.

One portion equals:
1 fat + 1 bread + 1 fruit.

164 kilocalories   4 g proteins   29 g carbohydrates   5 g fat
24 mg cholesterol   3 g fiber   1 mg iron   50 mg calcium
44 mg magnesium   229 mg potassium   95 mg sodium

Blueberry Muffins

Preparation time: 10 minutes   Cooking time: 20 minutes
12 servings

Egg	1	
Butter, non hydrogenated margarine, or oil	60 ml	(1/4 cup)
Brown sugar, sugar, honey, fructose or fruit purée	80 ml	(1/3 cup)
Blueberries, frozen or fresh	500 ml	(2 cups)
Nutmeg	2 ml	(1/2 tsp.)
Poppyseeds	15 ml	(1 tbsp.)
Salt	a pinch	
Milk (2% m.f. or less)	125 ml	(1/2 cup)
Flour, whole wheat with kamut flour, rye or oat flour . . .	500 ml	(2 cups)
Baking powder	15 ml	(1 tbsp.)

1. Mix the first 8 ingredients with a mixer by adding them one by one in the order indicated.
2. In another bowl, mix the flour (2 choices if possible) and baking powder together.
3. Add this mixture to the first mixture and stir lightly until it is homogeneous.
4. Fill a lightly greased pan for 12 muffins.
5. Bake in the oven at 200ºC (400ºF) for approx. 15-20 minutes.
6. Serve.

One portion equals:
1 fat + 1 bread + 1 fruit.

158 kilocalories   4 g proteins   25 g carbohydrates   5 g fat
29 mg cholesterol   4 g fiber   1 mg iron   65 mg calcium
35 mg magnesium   131 mg potassium   118 mg sodium

Bran Muffins

Preparation time: 10 minutes   Cooking time: 20 minutes
12 servings

Egg	1	
Butter, non hydrogenated margarine, or oil	60 ml	(1/4 cup)
Molasses	125 ml	(1/2 cup)
Dates, dried, puréed or in small pieces	60 ml	(1/4 cup)
Wheat bran	375 ml	(1 1/2 cups)
Salt	a pinch	
Milk (2% m.f. or less)	250 ml	(1 cup)
Flour, whole wheat	250 ml	(1 cup)
Baking powder	15 ml	(1 tbsp.)

1. Mix the first 7 ingredients with a mixer by adding them one by one in the order indicated.
2. In another bowl, mix the flour and baking powder together.
3. Add this mixture to the first mixture and stir lightly until it is homogeneous.
4. Fill a lightly greased pan for 12 muffins.
5. Bake in the oven at 200ºC (400ºF) for approx. 15-20 minutes.
6. Serve.

One portion equals:
1 fat + 1 bread + 1 fruit.

153 kilocalories   4 g proteins   27 g carbohydrates   5 g fat
30 mg cholesterol   5 g fiber   2 mg iron   98 mg calcium
100 mg magnesium   408 mg potassium   128 mg sodium

Orange Muffins

Preparation time: 10 minutes   Cooking time: 20 minutes
12 servings

Egg	1	
Butter, non hydrogenated margarine, or oil	60 ml	(1/4 cup)
Brown sugar, sugar, honey, fructose or fruit purée	80 ml	(1/3 cup)
Almond extract or vanilla extract	5 ml	(1 tsp.)
Orange, peeled and in pieces	3	
Salt	a pinch	
Milk (2% m.f. or less)	125 ml	(1/2 cup)
Flour, whole wheat with kamut flour, rye or oat flour	500 ml	(2 cups)
Baking powder	15 ml	(1 tbsp.)

1. Mix the first 7 ingredients with a mixer by adding them one by one in the order indicated.
2. In another bowl, mix the flour (2 choices if possible) and baking powder together.
3. Add this mixture to the first mixture and stir lightly until it is homogeneous.
4. Fill a lightly greased pan for 12 muffins.
5. Bake in the oven at 200°C (400°F) for approx. 15-20 minutes.
6. Serve.

One portion equals:
1 fat + 1 bread + 1 fruit.

156 kilocalories   4 g proteins   26 g carbohydrates   5 g fat
29 mg cholesterol   3 g fiber   1 mg iron   66 mg calcium
35 mg magnesium   170 mg potassium   117 mg sodium

Whole Grain Bread

Preparation time: 2 hours   Cooking time: 40 minutes
24 servings

Yeast, active, dry, fast, and instant	30 ml	(2 tbsps.)
Flour, whole wheat for bread	500 ml	(2 cups)
White flour, sifted, or rye flour	500 ml	(2 cups)
Salt	a pinch	
Butter, non hydrogenated margarine, or oil	30 ml	(2 tbsps.)
Milk (2% m.f. or less), hot but not boiling or water . .	500 ml	(2 cups)

WITH CHEESE : Add 250 ml (1 cup): cheddar, swiss, etc.
WITH FINE HERBS : Add 30 ml (2 tbsps.): basil, etc.
WITH SEEDS : Add 125 ml (1/2 cup): linseeds, sunflowers seeds, etc.
WITH VEGETABLES : Add 250 ml (1 cup): onion, etc.

1. Mix the first 4 ingredients.
2. Mix the other ingredients in another bowl.
3. Add this mixture to the first ingredients.
4. Add flour as needed until the dough is no longer sticky.
5. Knead for approx. 5 minutes. Put in a large pan.
6. Cover with a thin towel and let the dough rise to double its volume.
7. Punch the dough down, add your choice of ingredients.
8. Knead for approx. 8 minutes. Split in 2 portions.
9. Put in 2 greased bread pans and let rise for approx. 30 minutes.
10. Cook in the oven at 200°C (400°F) for approx. 35-40 minutes.
11. Remove from the mould, serve immediately or wrap each loaf.

One portion equals:
1 bread.

94 kilocalories   4 g proteins   17 g carbohydrates   2 g fat
4 mg cholesterol   3 g fiber   1 mg iron   34 mg calcium
33 mg magnesium   139 mg potassium   22 mg sodium

Pumpkin Bread

Preparation time: 15 minutes   Cooking time: 55 minutes
12 servings

Eggs	2	
Butter, non hydrogenated margarine, or oil	45 ml	(3 tbsps.)
Brown sugar, sugar, honey, fructose or fruit purée	30 ml	(2 tbsps.)
Pumpkin purée	250 ml	(1 cup)
Date purée or chocolate chips	125 ml	(1/2 cup)
Walnuts, chopped	60 ml	(1/4 cup)
Cinnamon, ground	2 ml	(1/2 tsp.)
Nutmeg, ground	2 ml	(1/2 tsp.)
Ginger, ground	5 ml	(1 tsp.)
Salt	a pinch	
Milk (2% m.f. or less)	60 ml	(1/4 cup)
Flour, whole wheat with kamut flour, rye or oat flour	500 ml	(2 cups)
Baking powder	15 ml	(1 tbsp.)

1. Mix the first 11 ingredients with a mixer by adding them one by one in the order indicated.
2. In another bowl, mix the flour (2 choices if possible) and baking powder together.
3. Add this mixture to the first mixture and stir lightly until it is homogeneous.
4. Put in a greased bread baking pan.
5. Bake in the oven at 180ºC (350ºF) for approx. 55-60 minutes.
6. Serve.

One portion equals:
1 fat + 1 bread + 1 fruit.

158 kilocalories   5 g proteins   24 g carbohydrates   6 g fat
44 mg cholesterol   3 g fiber   1 mg iron   53 mg calcium
38 mg magnesium   171 mg potassium   110 mg sodium

Molasses Flatcakes

Preparation time: 10 minutes   Cooking time: 20 minutes
12 servings

Egg	1	
Butter, non hydrogenated margarine, or oil	60 ml	(1/4 cup)
Molasses	125 ml	(1/2 cup)
Brown sugar, sugar, honey, fructose or fruit purée	60 ml	(1/4 cup)
Ginger, ground	2 ml	(1/2 tsp.)
Salt	a pinch	
Milk (2% m.f. or less)	60 ml	(1/4 cup)
Flour, whole wheat with kamut flour, rye or oat flour ..	500 ml	(2 cups)
Baking powder	15 ml	(1 tbsp.)

1. Mix the first 7 ingredients with a mixer by adding them one by one in the order indicated.
2. In another bowl, mix the flour (2 choices if possible) and baking powder together.
3. Add this mixture to the first mixture and stir lightly until it is homogeneous.
4. With a spoon, place 12 portions on a greased cookie sheet.
5. Flatten each cookie with damp fingers or with a floured fork.
6. Bake in the oven at 180°C (350°F) for approx. 15-20 minutes.
7. Serve.

One portion equals:
1 fat + 1 bread + 1 fruit.

171 kilocalories   4 g proteins   30 g carbohydrates   5 g fat
29 mg cholesterol   3 g fiber   2 mg iron   76 mg calcium
66 mg magnesium   314 mg potassium   120 mg sodium

117

Oatmeal and Raisin Cookies

Preparation time: 10 minutes   Cooking time: 20 minutes
12 servings

Egg	1	
Butter, non hydrogenated margarine, or oil	60 ml	(1/4 cup)
Brown sugar, sugar, honey, fructose or fruit purée	60 ml	(1/4 cup)
Vanilla	5 ml	(1 tsp.)
Raisins	125 ml	(1/2 cup)
Milk (2% m.f. or less)	125 ml	(1/2 cup)
Flour, whole wheat	250 ml	(1 cup)
Oatmeal, raw (oat flakes)	500 ml	(2 cups)
Baking powder	10 ml	(2 tsps.)

1. Mix the first 6 ingredients with a mixer in the order indicated.
2. In another bowl, mix the flour, oatmeal, and baking powder together.
3. Add this mixture to the first mixture and stir lightly until it is homogeneous.
4. With a spoon, place 12 portions on a greased cookie sheet.
5. Flatten each cookie with damp fingers or with a floured fork.
6. Bake in the oven at 180ºC (350ºF) for approx. 20 minutes.
7. Serve.

One portion equals:
1 fat + 1 bread + 1 fruit.

205 kilocalories   5 g proteins   34 g carbohydrates   6 g fat
29 mg cholesterol   3 g fiber   1 mg iron   52 mg calcium
45 mg magnesium   189 mg potassium   96 mg sodium

Date or Prune Squares

Preparation time: 10 minutes   Cooking time: 30 minutes
24 servings

Dates, dried or prunes, chopped	454 g	(1 pound)
Water	250 ml	(1 cup)
Lemon juice	5 ml	(1 tsp.)
Flour, whole wheat with kamut flour, rye or oat flour .	250 ml	(1 cup)
Oatmeal, raw	375 ml	(1 1/2 cups)
Salt	a pinch	
Brown sugar, sugar, honey, fructose or fruit purée . .	60 ml	(1/4 cup)
Butter, non hydrogenated margarine, or oil	30 ml	(2 tbsps.)
Water	80 ml	(1/3 cup)

1. Cook the dates or the prunes with water over moderate heat for approx. 15 minutes or until thickened.
2. Add the lemon juice.
3. Mix the other 6 ingredients in a bowl with a pastry cutter, a knife, or a fork.
4. Firmly press half the mixture into a greased square pan for the oven.
5. Spread the date or prune preparation on top.
6. Cover with the other half of the flour mixture.
7. Press with your fingers firmly but without crushing.
8. Bake in the oven at 180ºC (350ºF) for approx. 30 minutes.
9. Let cool and cut into 24 small squares.
10. Serve.

One portion equals:
1/2 fat + 1/2 bread + 1 fruit.

106 kilocalories   2 g proteins   23 g carbohydrates   2 g fat
3 mg cholesterol   3 g fiber   1 mg iron   11 mg calcium
23 mg magnesium   158 mg potassium   11 mg sodium

Apple Flatcakes

Preparation time: 10 minutes   Cooking time: 15 minutes
12 servings

Eggs, beaten	2	
Butter, non hydrogenated margarine, or oil	30 ml	(2 tbsps.)
Brown sugar, sugar, honey, fructose or fruit purée	80 ml	(1/3 cup)
Apples, in small pieces with peels	2	
Almonds, in pieces	60 ml	(1/4 cup)
Vanilla	5 ml	(1 tsp.)
Cinnamon	5 ml	(1 tsp.)
Milk (2% m.f. or less)	60 ml	(1/4 cup)
Flour, whole wheat with kamut flour, rye or oat flour	500 ml	(2 cups)
Baking powder	15 ml	(1 tbsp.)

1. Mix the first 8 ingredients with a mixer by adding them one by one in the order indicated.
2. In another bowl, mix the flour (2 choices if possible) and baking powder together.
3. Add this mixture to the first mixture and stir lightly until it is homogeneous.
4. With a spoon, place 12 portions on a greased cookie sheet.
5. Flatten each cookie with damp fingers or with a floured fork.
6. Bake in the oven at 180ºC (350ºF) for approx. 15-20 minutes.
7. Serve.

One portion equals:
1 fat + 1 bread + 1 fruit.

159 kilocalories   5 g proteins   26 g carbohydrates   5 g fat
42 mg cholesterol   3 g fiber   1 mg iron   59 mg calcium
41 mg magnesium   157 mg potassium   100 mg sodium

Cranberry Flatcakes

Preparation time: 10 minutes   Cooking time: 15 minutes
12 servings

Eggs	2	
Butter, non hydrogenated margarine, or oil	60 ml	(1/4 cup)
Brown sugar, sugar, honey, fructose or fruit purée	125 ml	(1/2 cup)
Cranberries, raw, fresh, cut in two	250 ml	(1 cup)
Orange juice	60 ml	(1/4 cup)
Salt	a pinch	
Vanilla	5 ml	(1 tsp.)
Milk (2% m.f. or less)	60 ml	(1/4 cup)
Flour, whole wheat with kamut flour, rye or oat flour	500 ml	(2 cups)
Baking powder	15 ml	(1 tbsp.)

1. Mix the first 8 ingredients with a mixer by adding them one by one in the order indicated.
2. In another bowl, mix the flour (2 choices if possible) and baking powder together.
3. Add this mixture to the first mixture and stir lightly until it is homogeneous.
4. With a spoon, place 12 portions on a greased cookie sheet.
5. Flatten each cookie with damp fingers or with a floured fork.
6. Bake in the oven at 180°C (350°F) for approx. 15-20 minutes.
7. Serve.

One portion equals:
1 fat + 1 bread + 1 fruit.

163 kilocalories   4 g proteins   26 g carbohydrates   5 g fat
47 mg cholesterol   3 g fiber   1 mg iron   49 mg calcium
32 mg magnesium   124 mg potassium   120 mg sodium

Apple and Cheese Pie

Preparation time: 10 minutes   Cooking time: 45 minutes
8 servings

HEALTHY PIE CRUST

Flour, whole wheat	500 ml	(2 cups)
Oil, non hydrogenated margarine, or butter	60 ml	(1/4 cup)
Yogurt, plain (2% m.f. or less)	180 ml	(3/4 cup)
Water	30 ml	(2 tbsps.)
Apples, in pieces	1.5 L	(6 cups)
Brown sugar, sugar, honey, fructose or fruit purée . .	30 ml	(2 tbsps.)
Flour of your choice	15 ml	(1 tbsp.)
Walnuts or other flavor	125 ml	(1/2 cup)
Cheddar cheese	125 ml	(1/2 cup)
Butter, non hydrogenated margarine, or oil	15 ml	(1 tbsp.)

1. Prepare the healthy pastry following the instructions on pg. 142.
2. Mix the 6 ingredients and put in the pastry.
3. Bake in the oven at 180ºC (350ºF) uncovered for approx. 45 minutes (apples cooked).
4. Remove from the oven and cool.

One portion equals:
1 meat + 2 fat + 2 breads + 1 fruit + 1 milk.

414 kilocalories   11 g proteins   54 g carbohydrates   20 g fat
23 mg cholesterol   7 g fiber   2 mg iron   184 mg calcium
71 mg magnesium   413 mg potassium   133 mg sodium

Apple Crisp Squares

Preparation time: 15 minutes   Cooking time: 30 minutes
12 servings

Flour, whole wheat with kamut flour, rye or oat flour .	250 ml	(1 cup)
Oatmeal, raw	375 ml	(1 1/2 cups)
Brown sugar, sugar, honey, fructose or fruit purée . .	60 ml	(1/4 cup)
Cinnamon	5 ml	(1 tsp.)
Nutmeg	a pinch	
Butter, non hydrogenated margarine, or oil	60 ml	(1/4 cup)
Water	80 ml	(1/3 cup)

Apples with peels, in small pieces 8

1. Mix the first 7 ingredients in a bowl with a pastry cutter.
2. Firmly press half the mixture into a greased square pan for the oven.
3. Add the apples cut into small pieces with the peel.
4. Cover with the other half of the flour mixture.
5. Press without crushing.
6. Bake in the oven at 180ºC (350ºF) for approx. 30 minutes.
7. Let cool and cut into 12 small squares.
8. Serve with a strained fruit purée of your choice (pg. 132).

One portion equals:
1 fat + 1 bread + 1 fruit.

191 kilocalories   4 g proteins   35 g carbohydrates   5 g fat
11 mg cholesterol   4 g fiber   1 mg iron   20 mg calcium
39 mg magnesium   201 mg potassium   41 mg sodium

Pear and Yogurt Cake Delight

Preparation time: 10 minutes   Cooking time: 60 minutes
12 servings

Egg	1	
Butter, non hydrogenated margarine, or oil	60 ml	(1/4 cup)
Brown sugar, sugar, honey, fructose or fruit purée .	60 ml	(1/4 cup)
Almond extract or vanilla extract	5 ml	(1 tsp.)
Flour, whole wheat with kamut flour, rye or oat flour	375 ml	(1 1/2 cups)
Baking powder	15 ml	(1 tbsp.)
Pear, fresh, in small pieces, with peel	4	
Flour, whole wheat	30 ml	(2 tbsps.)
Yogurt, plain (2% m.f. or less)	500 ml	(2 cups)
Almonds, in small pieces	60 ml	(1/4 cup)
Sugar, brown or white	60 ml	(1/4 cup)
Egg, beaten	1	
Lemon juice	5 ml	(1 tsp.)
Almond extract or vanilla extract	5 ml	(1 tsp.)

1. Mix the first 4 ingredients with a mixer by adding them one by one in the order indicated.
2. In another bowl, mix the flour (2 choices if possible) and baking powder together.
3. Add this mixture to the first mixture and stir lightly until it is homogeneous.
4. Press the mixture into a greased square baking pan.
5. Add the pears on top of this mixture.
6. Mix the other ingredients and add on top of the pears.
7. Bake in the oven at 180ºC (350ºF) for approx. 60-70 minutes.
8. Cut into 12 squares.
9. Serve cold or hot.

One portion equals:
1 fat + 1 bread + 1 fruit + 1/2 milk.

221 kilocalories   6 g proteins   33 g carbohydrates   8 g fat
51 mg cholesterol   4 g fiber   1 mg iron   124 mg calcium
44 mg magnesium   276 mg potassium   144 mg sodium

124

Chocolate or Carob Cake

Preparation time: 10 minutes   Cooking time: 25 minutes
12 servings

Eggs	2	
Butter, non hydrogenated margarine, or oil	60 ml	(1/4 cup)
Cocoa or carob, plain	180 ml	(3/4 cup)
Brown sugar, sugar, honey, fructose or fruit purée	125 ml	(1/2 cup)
Salt	a pinch	
Lemon juice	15 ml	(1 tbsp.)
Water	250 ml	(1 cup)
Milk (2% m.f. or less)	80 ml	(1/3 cup)
Flour, whole wheat with kamut flour, rye or oat flour	500 ml	(2 cups)
Baking powder	15 ml	(1 tbsp.)

1. Mix the first 8 ingredients with a mixer by adding them one by one in the order indicated.
2. In another bowl, mix the flour (2 choices if possible) and baking powder together.
3. Add this mixture to the first mixture and stir lightly until it is homogeneous.
4. Put in a greased square baking pan for the oven.
5. Bake in the oven at 180°C (350°F) for approx. 25-30 minutes.
6. Serve with the quick icing (pg. 131), strained fruit purée (pg. 132).

One portion equals:
1 fat + 1 bread + 1 fruit.

211 kilocalories   6 g proteins   37 g carbohydrates   6 g fat
48 mg cholesterol   3 g fiber   1 mg iron   99 mg calcium
44 mg magnesium   218 mg potassium   196 mg sodium

White Cake

Preparation time: 10 minutes   Cooking time: 25 minutes
12 servings

Eggs	2	
Butter, non hydrogenated margarine, or oil	60 ml	(1/4 cup)
Brown sugar, sugar, honey, fructose or fruit purée .	80 ml	(1/3 cup)
Salt	a pinch	
Vanilla	5 ml	(1 tsp.)
Milk (2% m.f. or less)	250 ml	(1 cup)
Flour, whole wheat with kamut flour, rye or oat flour	500 ml	(2 cups)
Baking powder	15 ml	(1 tbsp.)

1. Mix the first 6 ingredients with a mixer by adding them one by one in the order indicated.
2. In another bowl, mix the flour (2 choices if possible) and baking powder together.
3. Add this mixture to the first mixture and stir lightly until it is homogeneous.
4. Put in a greased square baking pan for the oven.
5. Bake in the oven at 180°C (350°F) for approx. 20-30 minutes.
6. Serve with the quick icing (pg. 131), strained fruit purée (pg. 132).

One portion equals:
1 fat + 1 bread + 1/2 fruit.

152 kilocalories   5 g proteins   22 g carbohydrates   6 g fat
48 mg cholesterol   3 g fiber   1 mg iron   68 mg calcium
33 mg magnesium   133 mg potassium   128 mg sodium

Carrot Cake

Preparation time: 10 minutes   Cooking time: 50 minutes
12 servings

Eggs	2	
Butter, non hydrogenated margarine, or oil	30 ml	(2 tbsps.)
Brown sugar, sugar, honey, fructose or fruit purée	80 ml	(1/3 cup)
Carrots, grated	500 ml	(2 cups)
Walnuts, chopped	60 ml	(1/4 cup)
Cinnamon	5 ml	(1 tsp.)
Salt	a pinch	
Vanilla	5 ml	(1 tsp.)
Milk (2% m.f. or less)	250 ml	(1 cup)
Flour, whole wheat with kamut flour, rye or oat flour	500 ml	(2 cups)
Baking powder	15 ml	(1 tbsp.)

1. Mix the first 9 ingredients with a mixer by adding them one by one in the order indicated.
2. In another bowl, mix the flour (2 choices if possible) and baking powder together.
3. Add this mixture to the first mixture and stir lightly until it is homogeneous.
4. Put in a greased square baking pan for the oven.
5. Bake in the oven at 180ºC (350ºF) for approx. 50 minutes.
6. Serve plain or with icing (pg. 131).

One portion equals:
1 fat + 1 bread + 1/2 fruit.

165 kilocalories   5 g proteins   27 g carbohydrates   5 g fat
43 mg cholesterol   4 g fiber   1 mg iron   82 mg calcium
43 mg magnesium   264 mg potassium   121 mg sodium

Apple and Raisin Cake

Preparation time: 10 minutes   Cooking time: 50 minutes
12 servings

Eggs	2	
Butter, non hydrogenated margarine, or oil	60 ml	(1/4 cup)
Brown sugar, sugar, honey, fructose or fruit purée	80 ml	(1/3 cup)
Apples with peels, in small pieces	2	
Raisins	60 ml	(1/4 cup)
Cinnamon	5 ml	(1 tsp.)
Nutmeg	2 ml	(1/2 tsp.)
Cloves, ground	a pinch	
Salt	a pinch	
Milk (2% m.f. or less)	250 ml	(1 cup)
Flour, whole wheat with kamut flour, rye or oat flour	500 ml	(2 cups)
Baking powder	15 ml	(1 tbsp.)

1. Mix the first 10 ingredients with a mixer by adding them one by one in the order indicated.
2. In another bowl, mix the flour (2 choices if possible) and baking powder together.
3. Add this mixture to the first mixture and stir lightly until it is homogeneous.
4. Put in a greased square baking pan for the oven.
5. Bake in the oven at 180ºC (350ºF) for approx. 50-60 minutes.
6. Serve plain, with apple sauce, a strained fruit purée (pg. 132), or with icing (pg. 131).

One portion equals:
1 fat + 1 bread + 1 fruit.

177 kilocalories   5 g proteins   29 g carbohydrates   6 g fat
48 mg cholesterol   3 g fiber   1 mg iron   74 mg calcium
36 mg magnesium   186 mg potassium   128 mg sodium

Strawberry Jam

Preparation time: 5 minutes   Cooking time: 4 minutes
16 servings

Gelatine, plain	1/3 envelope	(1 tsp.)
Water	45 ml	(3 tbsps.)
Brown sugar, sugar, honey, fructose or fruit purée .	30 ml	(2 tbsps.)
Strawberries, fresh	500 ml	(2 cups)
Water	15 ml	(1 tbsp.)
Zest of a lemon, grated	5 ml	(1 tsp.)

1. Sprinkle the gelatine onto the water and let swell for approx. 5 minutes.
2. Put the remaining ingredients in a pot and bring to a boil, approx. 2 minutes.
3. Mash the fruits with a pestle.
4. Add the swollen gelatine into the mixture and continue cooking for approx. 2 minutes.
5. Put in a jar and refrigerate.
6. Serve cold. Will keep for approx. 2 weeks in the refrigerator.

One portion equals:
1/2 fruit.

13 kilocalories   0 g protein   3 g carbohydrates   0 g fat
0 mg cholesterol   0 g fiber   0 mg iron   3 mg calcium
2 mg magnesium   37 mg potassium   1 mg sodium

Fruit Salad Cake

Preparation time: 10 minutes   Cooking time: 55 minutes
12 servings

Egg	1	
Butter, non hydrogenated margarine, or oil	60 ml	(1/4 cup)
Brown sugar, sugar, honey, fructose or fruit purée .	80 ml	(1/3 cup)
Fruit salad, not drained	398 ml	(1 x 14 oz can)
Almond extract or vanilla extract	5 ml	(1 tsp.)
Salt	a pinch	
Milk (2% m.f. or less)	125 ml	(1/2 cup)
Flour, whole wheat with kamut flour, rye or oat flour	500 ml	(2 cups)
Baking powder	15 ml	(1 tbsp.)

1. Mix the first 7 ingredients in a bowl as per the order indicated.
2. In another bowl, mix the flour (2 choices if possible) and baking powder together.
3. Add this mixture to the first mixture and stir lightly until it is homogeneous.
4. Put in a greased square baking pan.
5. Bake in the oven at 180°C (350°F) for approx. 50-60 minutes.
6. Serve plain, with a strained fruit purée (pg. 132), or with icing (pg. 131).

One portion equals:
1 fat + 1 bread + 1 fruit.

158 kilocalories   4 g proteins   26 g carbohydrates   5 g fat
29 mg cholesterol   3 g fiber   1 mg iron   56 mg calcium
34 mg magnesium   152 mg potassium   119 mg sodium

Quick Icing

Preparation time: 7 minutes   Cooking time: none
12 servings

VANILLA, ALMOND, MAPLE, OR LEMON FLAVOR

Cream cheese, light . . . .   60 ml   (1/4 cup)
Brown sugar, sugar, honey, fructose or fruit purée .   30 ml   (2 tbsps.)
Extract of your choice . . . .   2 ml   (1/2 tsp.)

CHOCOLATE OR CAROB FLAVOR

Carob chips or chocolate chips . . . .   60 ml   (1/4 cup)
Yogurt, plain (2% m.f. or less) . . . .   15 ml   (1 tbsp.)

1. Mix all ingredients for the desired icing.
2. Melt in small pot or in the microwave oven for 30-50 seconds.
3. Mix well.
4. Ice the cakes (or other desserts) as desired.

One portion equals:
Bonus if 5 ml (1 tsp.) or less.

24 kilocalories   1 g protein   3 g carbohydrates   1 g fat
4 mg cholesterol   0 g fiber   0 mg iron   13 mg calcium
1 mg magnesium   18 mg potassium   38 mg sodium

Strained Fruit Purée

Preparation time: 7 minutes   Cooking time: 5 minutes
4 servings

Strawberries, fresh, or other fruits or berries . . .	500 ml	(2 cups)
Brown sugar, sugar, honey, fructose or fruit purée .	30 ml	(2 tbsps.)
Water	30 ml	(2 tbsps.)

1. Cook all ingredients for approx. 5 minutes.
2. Put the mixture through a strainer.
3. Put in a container and refrigerate.
4. Serve with your favorite desserts.

One portion equals:
1 fruit.

50 kilocalories   1 g protein   12 g carbohydrates   0 g fat
0 mg cholesterol   2 g fiber   0 mg iron   12 mg calcium
9 mg magnesium   146 mg potassium   1 mg sodium

Homemade Plain Yogurt

Preparation time: 6 minutes   Cooking time: 15 minutes
6 servings

Gelatine, plain	1 envelope	(1 tbsp.)
Milk (2% m.f. or less)	1.0 L	(4 cups)
Skim milk powder	60 ml	(1/4 cup)
Yogurt, plain (2% m.f. or less)	125 ml	(1/2 cup)
Brown sugar, sugar, honey, fructose or fruit purée .	30 ml	(2 tbsps.)

1. Intersperse the gelatine in some milk (60 ml) and let swell for approx. 5 minutes.
2. Heat the rest of the milk and the milk powder to 82°C (180°F) in a double-boiler.
3. Add the gelatine to the hot mixture to dissolve. Mix.
4. Cool the liquid to 46°C (115°F), calculate approx. 45 minutes.
5. Add the yogurt, or culture (5g), and mix together.
6. Put in a pan and cover.
7. Put in the turned-off oven with the light on (60 watts).
8. Set aside for approx. 6 hours or overnight.
9. If there is water on top, use the electric mixer for a uniform texture.
10. Refrigerate and serve.

One portion equals:
1 milk.

139 kilocalories   10 g proteins   16 g carbohydrates   4 g fat
16 mg cholesterol   0 g fiber   0 mg iron   308 mg calcium
33 mg magnesium   406 mg potassium   128 mg sodium

Apple Delight

Preparation time: 70 minutes   Cooking time: none
6 servings

Gelatine, plain	1 envelope	(1 tbsp.)
Fruit juice of your choice	60 ml	(1/4 cup)
Lemon juice	15 ml	(1 tbsp.)
Apples with peels, in small pieces	2	
Fruit yogurt (2% m.f. or less) of your choice . . .	500 ml	(2 cups)
Walnuts or almonds, in pieces	10 ml	(2 tsps.)
Wheat germ	15 ml	(1 tbsp.)
Cinnamon	a pinch	

1. Sprinkle the gelatine onto the juice and let swell for approx. 5 minutes.
2. Heat to dissolve the gelatine (over low heat or in the microwave).
3. Pour the lemon juice on the apples to prevent them browning.
4. Mix the apples, yogurt, and nuts in another bowl.
5. Incorporate the dissolved gelatine and mix well.
6. Put in the dessert cups.
7. Refrigerate for at least 1 hour or until firm.
8. When ready to serve, sprinkle with wheat germ and cinnamon.

One portion equals:
1 fruit + 1/2 milk.

131 kilocalories   5 g proteins   24 g carbohydrates   2 g fat
5 mg cholesterol   1 g fiber   0 mg iron   111 mg calcium
16 mg magnesium   225 mg potassium   46 mg sodium

Yogurt Varieties

Preparation time: 5 minutes   Cooking time: none
1 serving

Yogurt, plain (2% m.f. or less) (pg. 133)	180 ml	(3/4 cup)
Fruit of your choice	30 ml	(2 tbsps.)
Linseeds (flaxseeds), ground	5 ml	(1 tsp.)

1. Mix ingredients.
2. For flavoured yogurt, add 1 ml (1/4 tsp.) of your choice of extract (vanilla, mint, almond, banana, maple, or of coffee and plain cocoa for a moka flavour.
3. Serve.

One portion equals:
1 milk.

143 kilocalories   9 g proteins   16 g carbohydrates   5 g fat
185 mg cholesterol   1 g fiber   0 mg iron   301 mg calcium
31 mg magnesium   479 mg potassium   114 mg sodium

Healthy Yogurt Popsicles

Preparation time: 2 minutes   Cooking time: none
12 servings

Yogurt, plain (2% m.f. or less)	500 ml	(2 cups)
Fruit of your choice	125 ml	(1/2 cup)
Brown sugar, sugar, honey, fructose or fruit purée .	30 ml	(2 tbsps.)

1. Add the recipe to 12 popsicle containers.
2. Freeze.
3. Serve.

One portion equals:
1/2 milk.

42 kilocalories   2 g proteins   6 g carbohydrates   1 g fat
4 mg cholesterol   0 g fiber   0 mg iron   70 mg calcium   7 mg magnesium
117 mg potassium   26 mg sodium

Blancmange

Preparation time: 5 minutes   Cooking time: 15 minutes
4 servings

Cornstarch	45 ml	(3 tbsps.)
Milk (2% m.f. or less)	500 ml	(2 cups)
Brown sugar, sugar, honey, fructose or fruit purée .	30 ml	(2 tbsps.)
Vanilla or other extract	5 ml	(1 tsp.)

1. Mix the cornstarch with some milk.
2. Add the rest of the milk and the sugar. Mix well.
3. Cook in a double-boiler (preferably) over low heat, stirring constantly until thickened.
4. Let boil for approx. 2 minutes.
5. Let cool and add the vanilla.
6. Put in 4 dessert cups.
7. Refrigerate.
8. Serve.

One portion equals:
1/2 fruit + 1/2 milk.

114 kilocalories   4 g proteins   18 g carbohydrates   2 g fat
10 mg cholesterol   0 g fiber   0 mg iron   157 mg calcium
18 mg magnesium   200 mg potassium   65 mg sodium

Fruity Snow of Your Choice

Preparation time: 130 minutes   Cooking time: none
6 servings

Gelatine, plain	1 envelope	(1 tbsp.)
Water	60 ml	(1/4 cup)
Egg whites, very fresh	4	
Brown sugar, sugar, honey, fructose or fruit purée . .	60 ml	(1/4 cup)
Strawberries, fresh, in pieces or raspberries, blueberries .	500 ml	(2 cups)

1. Sprinkle the gelatine onto the water and let swell for approx. 5 minutes.
2. Heat to dissolve the gelatine (over low heat or in the microwave).
3. Beat the egg whites into stiff peaks.
4. Gradually add the sugar and your choice of fruit.
5. Continue to beat and add the dissolved gelatine.
6. Put in 6 dessert cups and refrigerate for 2 hours.
7. Serve the same day if possible.
8. Top with a fresh strawberry or raspberry.

One portion equals:
1/2 meat + 1 fruit.

64 kilocalories   4 g proteins   12 g carbohydrates   0 g fat
0 mg cholesterol   1 g fiber   0 mg iron   10 mg calcium
9 mg magnesium   129 mg potassium   39 mg sodium

Tapioca Pudding

Preparation time: 5 minutes   Cooking time: 10 minutes
4 servings

Milk (2% m.f. or less)	500 ml	(2 cups)
Egg yolk, beaten	1	
Brown sugar, sugar, honey, fructose or fruit purée . .	30 ml	(2 tbsps.)
Salt	a pinch	
Tapioca, minute	45 ml	(3 tbsps.)
Vanilla	5 ml	(1 tsp.)

1. Mix the first 5 ingredients.
2. Put aside for approx. 5 minutes.
3. Cook in a double-boiler (preferably) over low heat, stirring constantly until thickened.
4. Remove from the heat and add the vanilla.
5. Put in 4 dessert cups.
6. Refrigerate.
7. Serve.

One portion equals:
1/2 bread + 1/2 fruit + 1/2 milk.

130 kilocalories   5 g proteins   19 g carbohydrates   4 g fat
64 mg cholesterol   0 g fiber   0 mg iron   164 mg calcium
18 mg magnesium   205 mg potassium   66 mg sodium

Fruit Jelly

Preparation time: 5 minutes   Cooking time: 60 minutes
6 servings

Gelatine, plain	1 envelope	(1 tbsp.)
Orange juice concentrate	180 ml	(3/4 cup)
Water	500 ml	(2 cups)

1. Sprinkle the gelatine onto the juice concentrate and let swell for approx. 5 minutes.
2. Heat to dissolve the gelatine (over low heat or in the microwave).
3. Add water to this mixture and stir well.
4. Put in the dessert cups and add fruit if desired.
5. Refrigerate.
6. Serve.

One portion equals:
1 fruit.

61 kilocalories   2 g proteins   14 g carbohydrates   0 g fat
0 mg cholesterol   0 g fiber   0 mg iron   12 mg calcium
13 mg magnesium   243 mg potassium   3 mg sodium

140

Plain Custard

Preparation time: 5 minutes   Cooking time: 45 minutes
4 servings

Eggs, beaten	2	
Brown sugar, sugar, honey, fructose or fruit purée . .	30 ml	(2 tbsps.)
Salt	a pinch	
Vanilla	1 ml	(1/4 tsp.)
Milk (2% m.f. or less)	250 ml	(1 cup)
Nutmeg	to your taste	

1. Mix all ingredients.
2. Pour into 4 dessert cups.
3. Put water (3 cm) in the bottom of a square pan.
4. Put the dessert cups in the pan.
5. Cover the dessert cups with a sheet of aluminum foil.
6. Bake in the oven at 180ºC (350ºF) for approx. 45 minutes.
7. Serve plain, with a strained fruit purée (pg. 132), some maple syrup, or with fresh fruit.

One portion equals:
1/2 meat + 1/2 fruit + 1/4 milk.

93 kilocalories   5 g proteins   10 g carbohydrates   4 g fat
11 mg cholesterol   0 g fiber   0 mg iron   91 mg calcium
11 mg magnesium   130 mg potassium   64 mg sodium

141

Infallible Pie Crust

Preparation time: 5 minutes   Cooking time: 10 minutes
12 servings

Flour, whole wheat or rye	500 ml	(2 cups)
Butter, non hydrogenated margarine, or oil	60 ml	(1/4 cup)
Yogurt, plain (2% m.f. or less)	180 ml	(3/4 cup)
Water	30 ml	(2 tbsps.)

1. Mix all ingredients.
2. Form into 2 balls.
3. Roll the pastry dough on a floured surface or between 2 sheets of waxed paper.
4. Use uncooked or bake in the oven at 180ºC (350ºF) for approx. 10 minutes.

One portion equals:
1 fat + 1 bread.

117 kilocalories   4 g proteins   16 g carbohydrates   5 g fat
12 mg cholesterol   3 g fiber   1 mg iron   33 mg calcium
32 mg magnesium   122 mg potassium   50 mg sodium

Fruity Cantaloupe

Preparation time: 20 minutes   Cooking time: none
4 servings

Cantaloupe, cut in 2, remove seeds 2
Sherbet, frozen yogurt, or iced milk . . . . 250 ml   (1 cup)

Fruit of your choice . . . . 250 ml   (1 cup)

1. Add a scoop of sherbet, iced milk, or frozen yogurt to the middle of the half cantaloupe.
2. Add fruit (kiwi, clementine, pear, apple, strawberry, etc.) on top.
3. Serve with a decorative cookie or a mint leaf.

One portion equals:
2 fruits.

120 kilocalories   3 g proteins   29 g carbohydrates   1 g fat
0 mg cholesterol   3 g fiber   1 mg iron   33 mg calcium
33 mg magnesium   940 mg potassium   24 mg sodium

Lemon Pie

Preparation time: 10 minutes   Cooking time: 5 minutes
6 servings

HEALTHY PIE CRUST

Flour, whole wheat	500 ml	(2 cups)
Oil, non hydrogenated margarine, or butter	60 ml	(1/4 cup)
Yogurt, plain (2% m.f. or less)	180 ml	(3/4 cup)
Water	30 ml	(2 tbsps.)
Lemon juice	125 ml	(1/2 cup)
Cornstarch	80 ml	(1/3 cup)
Water	430 ml	(1 3/4 cups)
Orange zest	5 ml	(1 tsp.)
Egg yolk, beaten	2	
Brown sugar, sugar, honey, fructose or fruit purée . . .	125 ml	(1/2 cup)
Egg white	2	
Sugar	30 ml	(2 tbsps.)

1. Prepare the healthy pastry following the instructions on pg. 142.
2. Mix the 4 ingredients and put in a saucepan.
3. Cook over medium heat stirring until thickened.
4. Remove from heat.
5. Mix the egg yolks with some of the hot mixture.
6. Pour into a saucepan stirring continually.
7. Bring to a boil until thickened.
8. Remove from the heat and add the lemon juice and zest.
9. Beat the egg whites until stiff (soft peaks), gradually adding the sugar.
10. Cool slightly and pour the topping into the cooked undercrust.
11. Spread the whites onto the topping up to the undercrust.
12. Brown lightly in the oven at 220ºC (425ºF) for 4 to 5 minutes.
13. Let cool and refrigerate. Serve.

One portion equals:
1/2 fat + 1 bread + 1 fruit.

387 kilocalories   9 g proteins   63 g carbohydrates   13 g fat
75 mg cholesterol   6 g fiber   2 mg iron   76 mg calcium
67 mg magnesium   291 mg potassium   45 mg sodium

Light Cheese Cake

Preparation time: 130 minutes   Cooking time: 25 minutes
8 servings

GRAHAM PIE CRUST

Breadcrumbs, Graham	250 ml	(1 cup)
Water	30 ml	(2 tbsps.)
Butter, non hydrogenated margarine, or oil	60 ml	(1/4 cup)

TOPPING

Gelatine, plain	1 envelope	(1 tbsp.)
Milk (2% m.f. or less)	60 ml	(1/4 cup)
Cream cheese, light	250 g	(1 packet)
Yogurt, plain (2% m.f. or less)	250 ml	(1 cup)
Lemon juice	30 ml	(2 tbsps.)
Brown sugar, sugar, honey, fructose or fruit purée	80 ml	(1/3 cup)
Vanilla	5 ml	(1 tsp.)
Fruit of your choice, fresh	250 ml	(1 cup)

1. Mix the first 3 ingredients and press into an 8 inch hinged mold.
2. Bake the crust in the oven at 180°C (350°F) for approx. 10 minutes.
3. Set aside.
4. Sprinkle the gelatine onto the milk and let swell for approx. 5 minutes.
5. Heat to dissolve the gelatine (over low heat or in the microwave).
6. Add the next 5 ingredients to this mixture.
7. Mix well.
8. Pour this mixture into the cooked pie shell.
9. Top with fresh fruit: kiwis, clementines, grapes, etc.
10. Allow to set for approx. 2 hours in the refrigerator.
11. Cut and serve.

One portion equals:
1/4 meat + 1 1/2 fat + 1 fruit + 1/3 milk.

230 kilocalories   6 g proteins   20 g carbohydrates   14 g fat
39 mg cholesterol   0 g fiber   0 mg iron   95 mg calcium
10 mg magnesium   152 mg potassium   366 mg sodium

No-Bake Treats

Preparation time: 70 minutes   Cooking time: 20 minutes
16 servings

Brown sugar, sugar, honey, fructose or fruit purée .	60 ml	(1/4 cup)
Peanuts	125 ml	(1/2 cup)
Oatmeal, raw	500 ml	(2 cups)
Carob chips or chocolate chips	60 ml	(1/4 cup)
Raisins	60 ml	(1/4 cup)
Peanut butter	250 ml	(1 cup)
Water	80 ml	(1/3 cup)
Carob chips or chocolate chips	60 ml	(1/4 cup)
Milk (2% m.f. or less)	15 ml	(1 tbsp.)

1. Mix the first 7 ingredients.
2. Put in a square baking pan and press down firmly with fingers.
3. Melt the chips with the milk and spread over the first mixture.
4. Refrigerate for 1 hour, cut, and serve.

One portion equals:
1 meat + 1 1/2 fat + 1/2 bread + 1 fruit.

205 kilocalories   8 g proteins   19 g carbohydrates   12 g fat
1 mg cholesterol   3 g fiber   1 mg iron   29 mg calcium
57 mg magnesium   231 mg potassium   86 mg sodium

Fruit Salad

Preparation time: 10 minutes   Cooking time: none
8 servings

Red apple, in pieces 1
Kiwi, in pieces 1
Cantaloupe, in balls 1
Banana, in round slices 1
Grapes, red or green, seedless 15
Pear, fresh, in pieces 1

Fruit juice of your choice . . . . 250 ml   (1 cup)

1. Mix all ingredients.
2. Serve.

One portion equals:
1 fruit.

88 kilocalories   1 g protein   22 g carbohydrates   1 g fat
0 mg cholesterol   2 g fiber   0 mg iron   18 mg calcium
18 mg magnesium   383 mg potassium   8 mg sodium

Rice Pudding

Preparation time: 5 minutes   Cooking time: 10 minutes
6 servings

Milk (2% m.f. or less)	500 ml	(2 cups)
Cornstarch	45 ml	(3 tbsps.)
Brown sugar, sugar, honey, fructose or fruit purée . .	60 ml	(1/4 cup)
Vanilla	2 ml	(1/2 tsp.)
Brown rice, long grain, cooked	500 ml	(2 cups)
Nutmeg or cinnamon	to your taste	

1. Mix the milk, cornstarch and sugar.
2. Cook in a double-boiler (preferably) over low heat, stirring constantly until thickened.
3. Remove from the heat and add the vanilla.
4. Add this mixture to the rice and mix well.
5. Put in 4 dessert cups.
6. Sprinkle lightly with nutmeg or cinnamon.
7. Refrigerate.
8. Serve.

One portion equals:
1 bread + 1 fruit + 1/3 milk.

167 kilocalories   5 g proteins   32 g carbohydrates   2 g fat
6 mg cholesterol   1 g fiber   0 mg iron   112 mg calcium
41 mg magnesium   163 mg potassium   47 mg sodium

Fruit Dip

Preparation time: 10 minutes   Cooking time: none
4 servings

Yogurt, plain (2% m.f. or less)	125 ml	(1/2 cup)
Cream cheese, light	125 ml	(1/2 cup)
Brown sugar, sugar, honey, fructose or fruit purée .	30 ml	(2 tbsps.)
Fruit juice (orange, tropical, etc.)	15 ml	(1 tbsp.)
Fruit of your choice, in pieces	4	
Lemon juice	15 ml	(1 tbsp.)
Walnuts, chopped	5 ml	(1 tsp.)

1. Mix the first 4 ingredients.
2. Put on a dip platter.
3. Mix the fruit pieces with lemon juice to prevent them browning.
4. Arrange around the dip platter.
5. Sprinkle with chopped nuts.
6. Serve.

One portion equals:
1 fat + 1 fruit + 1/2 milk.

160 kilocalories   5 g proteins   20 g carbohydrates   7 g fat
22 mg cholesterol   2 g fiber   0 mg iron   86 mg calcium
13 mg magnesium   304 mg potassium   234 mg sodium

Bavarian Pineapple Delight

Preparation time: 70 minutes   Cooking time: none
4 servings

Gelatine, plain	1 envelope	(1 tbsp.)
Pineapple juice	60 ml	(1/4 cup)
Pineapple pieces with juice	540 ml	(1 x 19 oz can)
Yogurt, plain (2% m.f. or less)	250 ml	(1 cup)
Brown sugar, sugar, honey, fructose or fruit purée	60 ml	(1/4 cup)
Coconut (optional)	60 ml	(1/4 cup)

1. Sprinkle the gelatine onto the pineapple juice and let swell for approx. 5 minutes.
2. Heat this mixture to dissolve the gelatine.
3. Add the gelatine to the remaining ingredients and mix.
4. Put in 4 dessert cups and refrigerate for at least 1 hour.
5. Serve.

One portion equals:
1 fat + 2 fruits + 1/2 milk.

266 kilocalories   6 g proteins   44 g carbohydrates   9 g fat
6 mg cholesterol   3 g fiber   1 mg iron   131 mg calcium
39 mg magnesium   416 mg potassium   49 mg sodium

Other

Information

Harmonie Santé Healthy Plate

Here is an example of the healthy plate, which you can apply almost anywhere (restaurants, friends, home, lunches, etc.). Half of the plate is filled with vegetables, a quarter with the meats and alternatives group, and the other quarter with breads and cereal products (rice, pasta, bread, etc.).

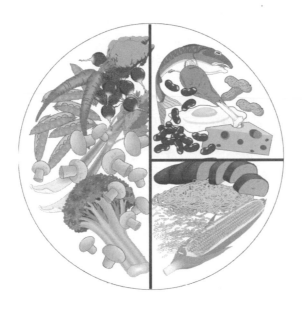

As a snack or for dessert: have a fruit and a milk product (milk, yogurt, cheese, etc.), or, on occasion, a small dessert (one quarter of a dessert plate).

For a nutrition evaluation and personalised advice, do not hesitate to meet with a nutritionist who is a member of the *Harmonie Santé Group* nearest you. The Food Agenda/Agenda alimentaire from the *"Harmonie Santé"* collection, may also be a useful tool to help you modify your eating habits. Enjoy your meals!

Food Equivalents

To help you eat in a well-balanced way throughout the day, the food equivalents for each recipe have been calculated in order to give you a general outline of their contents. They are divided into six food groups. Within the same group we find foods having similar characteristics and nutritive values. A balanced intake means that food from each of these groups should be included based on the suggested equivalents below. It is, however, important to note that these amounts are not fixed and may vary from one person to another or from one day to another. The suggested quantities respect the recommendations of Canada's Food Guide but the system used to calculate the food equivalents proposed here is different.

IT IS SUGGESTED THAT PEOPLE CONSUME EACH DAY:

- 5 TO 9 SERVINGS OF MEATS AND ALTERNATIVES.
  2 to 4 meats and alternatives are equal to about one quarter of a plate.

- 3 TO 7 SERVINGS OF VEGETABLES.
  Choose fresh vegetables and wash them well.

- 3 TO 5 SERVINGS OF FAT.
  We should not completely remove fat from our diets; they are even essential for those wanting to lose body fat and be in better shape.

- 5 TO 12 SERVINGS OF BREADS AND CEREALS.
  1 to 2 breads and cereals are equal to about one quarter of a plate.

- 2 TO 5 SERVINGS OF FRUIT.
  Choose fresh fruit and wash them well.

- 2 TO 4 SERVINGS OF MILK AND MILK PRODUCTS PER DAY.
  Milk and milk products and exercise are essential to keep our bones in good shape.

Menu Suggestions

Here are several ideas for combining appetizers, main dishes, side dishes, and desserts to help you create your menus. Be imaginative. Do not hesitate to vary your menus by interchanging the proposed choices while keeping in mind the characteristics of each dish. For example, you can have your dessert with a milk product a little later after the meal. Ensure your appetite is satisfied without feeling too full.

Menu 1
Stuffed Zucchini (pg.1)
Fettuccini Alfredo (pg. 101)
Caesar Salad (pg. 22)
Date or Prune Squares (pg. 119)

Menu 2
Cheese-Stuffed Mushrooms (pg. 2)
Wrapped Fish Fillets (pg. 94)
Sweet Potato
Broccoli
Lemon Pie (pg. 144)

Menu 3
Cheese Bites (pg. 3)
Chinese Tofu (pg. 73)
Rice
Fruit Dip (pg. 149)

Menu 4
Salmon Mousse (pg. 4)
Meat Brochette (pg. 67)
Rice
Greek Salad (pg. 23)
Blancmange (pg. 137)

Menu 5
Light Cretons (pg. 5)
Chicken Stew (pg. 63)
Bread
Bavarian Pineapple Delight (pg. 150)

Menu 6
Vegetable Soup (pg. 11)
Meatloaf Feast (pg. 46)
Vegetables with Melted Cheese (pg. 76)
Light Cheese Cake (pg. 145)

Menu 7
Pea Soup (pg.13)
Meatball Stew (pg. 87)
Mashed Potato
Julienne-cut Carrots
Fruity Cantaloupe (pg. 143)

Menu 8
French Onion Soup (pg.14)
Curried Pork Cutlets (pg. 81)
Rice
Blancmange (pg. 137)

Menu 9
Lentil Soup (pg. 15)
Vegetarian Hamburger (pg. 74)
Hamburger Bun
Coleslaw (pg. 26)
Fruit Jelly (pg. 140)

Menu 10
Cream of Carrot Soup (pg. 17)
Coquilles Saint-Jacques (pg. 97)
Bread
Caesar Salad (pg. 22)
Plain custard (pg. 141)

Menu 11
Cream of Vegetable Soup (pg. 18)
Salmon Loaf (pg. 96)
Rice
Broccoli
Tapioca Pudding (pg. 139)

Menu 12
Cream of Tomato Soup (pg. 19)
Quiche Lorraine (pg. 85)
Tasty Salad (pg. 28)
Fruit Salad Cake (pg. 130)

Menu 13
Chicken Salad (pg. 21)
Sandwiches (pg. 86)
Vegetables with Dip (pg. 31)
Yogurt Varieties (pg. 135)

Menu 14
Caesar Salad (pg. 22)
Fillet of Sole with Almonds (pg. 92)
Rice
Apple and Cheese Pie (pg. 122)

Menu 15
Greek Salad (pg. 23)
Breaded Honey Chicken (pg. 61)
Baked Potato
Green Beans
Carrot Cake (pg. 127)

Legume Cooking

Legumes are rich in fiber and low in fat as well as economical. They are a good alternative to meat since they also contain protein. However, like all vegetable proteins, these are not complete. It is therefore necessary to ensure a daily intake of a wide variety of food from the food equivalents (pg. 152) to obtain the proteins required. You will save a lot of time if you prepare legumes in large amounts and freeze them in 1 cup (250 ml) bags. Here is a table to guide you when cooking legumes:

UNCOOKED LEGUMES 1 CUP (250 ml)	SOAKING (HOURS)	PRESSURE COOKING (MINUTES)	COOKING WATER	COOKING TIME (HOURS)	YIELD AFTER COOKING
LIMA BEANS	NONE	3	2 CUPS (500 ml)	1 1/2	1 1/2 CUPS (375 ml)
MUNG BEANS	NONE	15	3 CUPS (750 ml)	1 1/2	2 CUPS (500 ml)
KIDNEY BEANS	6 - 8	AVOID	3 CUPS (750 ml)	1 1/2	2 CUPS (500 ml)
SOYA BEANS	24	15	3 CUPS (750 ml)	3	2 CUPS (500 ml)
WHITE BEANS	6 - 8	25 - 45	3 CUPS (750 ml)	3	2 CUPS (500 ml)
LENTILS	NONE	AVOID	3 CUPS (750 ml)	1	2 1/4 CUPS (560 ml)
SPLIT PEAS	NONE	AVOID	3 CUPS (750 ml)	1	2 1/4 CUPS (560 ml)
CHICKPEAS	8	25 - 45	4 CUPS (1000 ml)	2 - 3	2 CUPS (500 ml)
SOUP PEAS	6 - 8	25 - 45	3 CUPS (750 ml)	3	2 CUPS (500 ml)

Source: Publication 1555, Agriculture Canada

Herbs and Spices

Herbs and spices are alternatives to salt. They flavor and heighten the taste of foods. Here is a table outlining how to use herbs, spices, and others.

USE OF HERBS	SPICES, AND OTHER SEASONINGS
ASPARAGUS	BASIL, CHIVES, DILL, LEMON JUICE, TARRAGON
BEEF	BASIL, CUMIN, CURRY, GARLIC, GINGER, BAY LEAF, MARJORAM, DRY MUSTARD, ONION, OREGANO, THYME
BROCCOLI, CABBAGE CAULIFLOWER	BASIL, CURRY, GARLIC, GINGER, MARJORAM, OREGANO, TARRAGON, THYME
CARROTS	CHIVES, CUMIN, MARJORAM, MINT, NUTMEG, PARSLEY, TARRAGON
EGGS	CHIVES, CURRY, CUMIN, TARRAGON, SAVORY
EGGPLANT	BASIL, GARLIC, MARJORAM, OREGANO, SAGE, THYME
FISH	CURRY, FENNEL, LEMON JUICE, DRY MUSTARD, PAPRIKA
LAMB	CURRY, DILL, GARLIC, MINT, OREGANO, ROSEMARY, THYME
MUSHROOMS	BASIL, CHIVES, DILL, GARLIC, ROSEMARY, TARRAGON
POTATO	CHIVES, CURRY, DILL, GARLIC, BAY LEAF, ONION, SAVORY
PORK	APPLE SAUCE, CORIANDER, CUMIN, CURRY, DILL, GARLIC, GINGER, ONION, ROSEMARY, SAGE, THYME
POULTRY	BASIL, CHIVES, CORIANDER, CURRY, GARLIC, GINGER, PAPRIKA, SAGE, TARRAGON, THYME
RICE	CHIVES, CUMIN, CURRY, GARLIC, SAGE, TARRAGON, THYME
SPINACH	BASIL, GARLIC, LEMON JUICE, NUTMEG, TARRAGON
TURNIP	CINNAMON, GINGER, NUTMEG
VEAL	CORIANDER, CURRY, DILL, GARLIC, BAY LEAF, LEMON JUICE, OREGANO, PAPRIKA, ROSEMARY, SAGE, THYME

NO-SALT SHAKER

Basil.	5 ml	(1 tsp)
Pepper.	5 ml	(1 tsp)
Paprika.	2 ml	(1/2 tsp)
Parsley	5 ml	(1 tsp)
Onion powder. . . .	5 ml	(1 tsp)
Garlic powder. . . .	2 ml	(1/2 tsp)

1. Mix all ingredients.
2. Put in a small spice container.
3. Use to replace salt in salads, soups, hot meals, etc.

Recipe Modifications

Here are some suggestions or possible substitutions to improve the nutritive value of your recipes or, quite simply, for variety.

- To have more fiber in your recipes, replace white flour with a mixture of rye flour, whole wheat flour, oat flour, or other flour. These flours are richer in fiber and provide an interesting texture to your muffins, cakes, biscuits, etc.

- Rice, potato, corn, and soy flours are used in cases of gluten intolerance since they are gluten-free. Ask your nutritionist to give you more suggestions for gluten-free recipe adjustments.

- Replace sugar or brown sugar with the same amount of puréed dates. Date purée contains fiber and has good nutritional value. You can also make fig or prune purées.

- Choose better quality fats: those rich in monounsaturated fatty acids such as olive oil, canola oil, avocado, nuts, and those rich in essential fatty acids such as linseeds (flaxseed) or linseed oil, fatty fish or fish oils. Good fats are essential for the proper functioning of the body. Choosing a good fat is important.

- Tofu is an excellent meat substitute. It is made from soybeans, contains less fat and a high quantity of vegetable protein. It is surprising and pleasing to discover the results when a half or more of the meat is replaced by tofu (crushed with a fork or cut into cubes) in a recipe in order to obtain a vegetarian or semi-vegetarian dish.

- Legumes are rich in dietary fiber, proteins, and nutritious elements. Cooked lentils can be used to replace the meat and are delicious in ground meat recipes (spaghetti sauce, beef delight, etc.).

Experiment with your recipe modifications, adding your own personal touch!

References and Bibliography

- Brault Dubuc, M. and L. Caron Lahaie. Valeur nutritive des aliments, Montreal, 1998.

- Frappier, Renée and Danielle Gosselin. Guide des bons gras. Les éditions Asclépiade, 1995.

- Frappier, Renée. Le guide de l'alimentation saine et naturelle. Les éditions Asclépiade, 1987.

- Kousmine, C. Soyez bien dans votre assiette jusqu'à 80 ans et plus. France, 1980.

- Lagacé-Lambert, Louise and Michelle Laflamme. Bons gras et mauvais gras. Les éditions de l'homme, 1993.

- Manuel de nutrition clinique. Ordre professionnel des diététistes du Québec, 2nd edition. 1991.

- Monette, Solange. Dictionnaire encyclopédique des aliments. Éditions Québec/Amérique, 1989.

- Health and Welfare Canada. Nutrition Recommendations. Montreal, 1983.

- Health and Welfare Canada. Canada's Food Guide Handbook. Montreal, 1992.

Comments

You can leave us your comments by calling us
at 514-990-7128 or at 1-877-HARMONIE
Write us at harmo.sa@videotron.ca
Visit our Web site: www.harmoniesante.com

Your comments :

_____

_____

_____

_____

_____

_____

_____

_____

_____

_____

_____

Harmonie Santé

Gifts For You and Your Friends

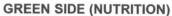

Tools to help you on the road ahead.

GREEN SIDE (NUTRITION)

Healthful recipe book developed by a nutritionist, entitled "*Healthy Eating Made Easy For The Whole Family*". This book contains easy-to-make healthful recipes. It is suitable for the whole family, for people with diabetes or with cardiovascular problems, and for those desiring to lose body fat or improve their eating habits. The food equivalents are indicated for each recipe. Also included in this book are menu examples, the healthy plate, legume cooking, recipe modifications, etc. Eating in a healthful way and with enjoyment is the basis for harmony.

RED SIDE (PHYSICAL ACTIVITIES)

Exercise video cassette "*Action Harmonie Santé*" (available in French only). At the beginning of the video, a nutritionist, a psychologist, and a physical educator introduce and describe the approach of the Harmonie Santé triangle. As well, with your doctor's permission, you can begin the 30 minutes of starter/intermediate-level exercises led by Chantal Cyr, physical educator.

YELLOW SIDE (SELF-ESTEEM)

A food agenda developed by nutritionists, entitled "*l'agenda alimentaire*" (currently available in French only), is a useful tool for those who are trying to make changes to their eating habits or to lose or maintain weight, while preserving the pleasure of good eating without guilt. It has proven to be a valuable tool when undertaking lifestyle changes and helps make people aware of everything consumed while making links with all that is accomplished in the course of a day.

To order these items, contact us at:

(514) 990-7128 or 1-877-HARMONIE or www.harmoniesante.com

Who Can Benefit From Our Services?

The nutritionists, members of the Harmonie Santé Group, have a respectful approach based on the Harmonie Santé triangle. Do not hesitate to consult them. Many insurance companies reimburse consultation fees. Here are the topics that can be discussed during our consultations:

- Allergies and intolerances
- Anemia
- Anorexia, bulimia, overeating
- Cancer
- Diabetes
- Digestive problems
- Diverticulosis/diverticulitis
- Gastrointestinal problems
- Gout
- High triglycerides
- Hypercholesterolemia
- Hypertension
- Hypoglycemia

- Irritable bowel
- Lack of energy
- Menu ideas, lunch box
- Nutrition: infant, child
- Nutrition: adolescent
- Nutrition: adult, senior
- Obesity
- Pregnancy and breastfeeding
- Slow digestion, bloating
- Sports nutrition
- Vegetarianism
- Weight loss and maintenance
- Weight gain

Meeting with a nutritionist is a profitable
investment for your health and your society!

Request advice from the nutritionists of the *Harmonie Santé Group*,
participants in the public health improvement project.
Contact us to learn more about the services we offer.

Visit our Web site :
www.harmoniesante.com
Head Office :
(514) 990-7128 or 1-877-HARMONIE

Your health starts with your food!